Knotted

By Andrea Hunt

Acknowledgements

Edited by Greg Helmerick and Renee Covino

Cover and Back Photography by

Armando Geneyro

@knoweroftheledge

Cover and Back Photography Assistant

Daniel Barrientos

Creative Contributions by

Panama Soweto,

Tyler Maez, and Brittney Morris

I asked my grandma, "If you could have done anything in your life, what would you have done?"

"I would have gone to beauty college."

Prologue

Yes, read the fucking prologue.

I am not writing this book because I think I am an exceptionally fascinating person, or that I have lived a life that is all that different from anyone else's. I just put fingers to keyboard, thoughts to fingers, and this is what happened.

I began writing this book when I got clean and sober in August of 2009. At the time, I needed an outlet. I needed something to pass the time as I avoided the triggers of addiction by isolating myself in my bedroom, staring at the same four walls night after night. At the time, I had been doing hair for around fifteen years, and thought I'd put together a book of my salon stories, and all of the ins and outs of the business. I wanted it to be kind of a behind-the-scenes book—or memoir, filled with funny anecdotes about clients and coworkers. As I began to write and really put thoughts into words, I realized that this book is more than a simple collection of career stories. These stories were my realities.

I also realized that for more time than I like to admit to, I lived a double life of sorts. I had hidden struggles that I always walked alone in silence. I had struggles and a dark existence that no one knew about. I was both a professional with a life that looked good on paper, as well as an addict and alcoholic. Many people are. But we keep that a secret for as long as we can. Until the shift finally happens, the balance of a professional life and the contrasting ugliness of addiction just become our normal. I know a few of you can relate.

More people than you or I know, live double lives, drowning in their own self-created murky waters; self-medicating with substance to clear the fog of past pain, only to bring in a different kind of fog that comes with an altered state of mind—and ultimately spirit. The cycle is endless. Until you end it.

decision not to have children at a very early age. Pursuing my career became my child. I saw how having kids at a young age robbed my parents of truly following their dreams. I wanted something more than a struggle to be my reality, much like life was for my parents. I chose a career and travel over a husband and children. I chose independence over obligation. I chose to make my life what I wanted it to be, despite the inevitable hurdles and challenges that I often created.

The stories I've chosen to include in this book do give an accurate account of my experience as a hairdresser standing behind the chair in the salon for two decades, as well as the situations that permanently changed me. And of course, these stories changed the course of my career and life. All names and places have been changed.

I had a wonderful career. I met some amazing and talented people. I learned from the best, and traveled and learned some more. Some of my clients became some of my closest friends. When you think about it, I saw my clients more often than I saw a lot of my family. When that happens, you become friends. You learn how to read each other. You can tell when the client is happy, and they could tell if I was happy. We could also read in each other if something upsetting happened. And, after some time, you become comfortable enough to talk about your lives and confide in each other.

When I think about it, all I really wanted to accomplish was to make my parents and grandparents proud of me. My teen years weren't easy. They were pretty traumatic, actually, and I always felt a push from within to prove everyone wrong and make them proud. I think the proudest moment I remember of my dad was when we had an opening party at a salon I worked at. He choked up at how beautiful the salon was and how far I'd come from my destructive past. He was especially proud when my sister and I modeled for a photo shoot for a salon I was working at, and the photos were published in a local magazine. I think my mom, dad, and grandparents bought every copy of the magazine they could afford and showed everyone who would look and listen to them.

Pot Pies

My career was filled with many personal and soul-defining ups and downs. Perhaps the most pivotal moment in my career—and in my life—was March 17, 2007. It was St. Patrick's Day. That year it happened to fall on a Saturday, which meant for people who work in the city, it was going to be a chaotic mess, full of people who are blacked-out drunk by noon. I had arranged to leave work around 2:45 p.m. All I wanted to do was finish up and get the fuck out of there. I had gone shopping at a local health-food store the evening prior, and stocked up on strip steaks and artichokes for the weekend. I had talked to my dad while I was shopping, and he had told me he had received some sort of recognition at work and was pretty excited about it. I told him congratulations. He sounded in good spirits. This was music to my ears.

I could tell this was one of his better moments since the breakup he had just gone through. I was trying to encourage him to get out more and eat better and that someone else that was way better would come along. I had also been inpatient with him because he sounded depressed and hopeless when talking about his ex-girlfriend. It was very frustrating. I just wanted my dad back and for him to get healthy. His now ex-girlfriend possessed an element of toxicity that polluted our entire family. Since she and my dad had started dating nine- years prior, his mental and physical health had plummeted. They had both taken an already high level of drinking and partying to an even more elevated status. His newfound interest in healthier eating made me hopeful that soon my dad would be back to himself, and I could have a role model I so desperately craved, but never voiced my feeling of father-figure void.

I woke up that morning in an unusual mood. I had been contemplating breaking up with my fiancé Derik. To say we had nothing in common was an understatement. I had reached the point in the relationship where I was imagining what my life would look like without him…without Caden. Caden was the child that was still in his life from a previous relationship. Now he was in our lives on a regular basis, as was Caden's mother, and this brought an entire dynamic to our relationship that was decreasingly welcome, at least by me. I had tried being open-minded and accommodating to the situation, and I was, but boundaries were regularly being crossed, and crossed boundaries lead to resentment. Resentment leads to anger, and anger destroys the bond in any relationship. Resentment is often the point of no return.

All I wanted to do was get to work and finish my day. I had just gotten home from a salon trip to Vegas. The salon had tickets for a trade show that was held annually in Vegas. I think our boss was the only person that was really into going to some of the classes and actually learning something at this event. The rest of us wanted to escape our lives and party into oblivion in the bars and clubs of Vegas. And that is what we did. I think I slept a total of six hours the whole time. In three days, we managed to eat at a few amazing restaurants, go to the show, sight-see, bar hop all over the place, score an ample amount of cocaine, and see a concert. Well, only a few of us went to a concert. But it was nothing short of cocaine-and vodka-fueled shit show that was blurry and messy and ugly.

I had returned to Denver a strung-out mess. The morning we left Vegas, a few of us stayed up all night snorting lines of cocaine into our faces. By 8 a.m., I thought I should take a nap before our 11 a.m. flight. Pamela had to wake me by shaking the shit out of me. I didn't have time to change or shower or brush my teeth; I literally threw everything in my carry-on and put on my dark sunglasses. Somehow I made it through the airport and through the flight without puking all over the place.

The post-cocaine depressions had been getting to me all week. I had been back for four days and still felt like shit from all the drinking, smoking, and snorting I did in Vegas. I was also bothered because our dad had been acting very strangely since he and his noxious girlfriend broke up. I didn't see why he was so down about it; the woman was an opportunist. I was actually excited for his sad and depressed phase to commence so we could have our dad back. Bernadette, his girlfriend, had been in the picture for nearly a decade. We had confirmed information regarding their once, stint, if you will, with cocaine. I was pretty sure it was over and that they had just gone a little too far in the bar scene. After all, my dad was fifty and one might think he would have been ready to put his party lifestyle behind him. But, he did love the nightlife. He and our mother had us when they were very young and they completely missed out on that phase of their lives. Once I turned fifteen and they were divorced, they started reliving what should have been. My mom eventually put an end to her partying, but my dad never did. He reveled in it.

I never knew any differently or any better when it came to my dad's, for that matter, all of my family's excessive drinking habits. I thought it was perfectly normal for my dad to have a shot of scotch and a cigarette before noon—or for a person to drink nothing but cheap beers common to poor college kids and alcoholics. That's it. No water; no juice; no tea: just beer. This is what I thought was normal and that everyone had parents who went out to the clubs on the weekends. Not that this is not normal, or right or wrong, it just was what it was. Derik had pointed out on a few occasions that maybe my dad should slow down on the drinking and smoking. My dad smoked at least a pack of non-filtered cigarettes every day. This had concerned me a lot, but smoking and having a beer together at some of my parties were all I felt I had in common with him at this point, even though it tore me up inside. So I would just drink and smoke. And when he came over or we were at a rare family gathering, we would drink and smoke together. It was our only bond.

My friend Spencer was scheduled as my last appointment that day for a haircut. I had purposely booked him as my last appointment because I honestly felt very at home when he was around. He always understood me, my humor, and always knew what I was thinking before I had to say it. Deep down, I knew that he would do anything for me and all I had to do was ask. We always had an indescribable affinity for each other. Not in a soulmate/lover/relationship way, but just as if we were two people that would always be in each other's lives no matter what.

As long as we had been friends, we had a connection. We dated when we were in our very early twenties. Our relationship began in the midst of a relationship I was trying to end with another person. Looking back, they were both dysfunctional relationships with unsuitable men. Well, I wasn't exactly a suitable person myself. I had put him through the ringer, not only once but twice. For some reason, after all these years we had remained friends and always picked up where we left off. I can't say if there was ever any deliberate flirtation or just a tension that was the spawn of both of us deep down wondering *what if?*

The tension and connection excited me when Spencer would come in, not because I didn't care about my fiancé, not because I was lusting after Spencer, but because I truly believe he is one person that will always have a piece of my emotions. He is familiar, he understands me as if he has known me since birth, and he listens. I could tell he knew I was unhappy, and I could tell that he could tell.

I was annoyed at Derik because he was going to get Caden and bring him over. Caden was the thorn in my side that caused most of our fights. Caden was his ex-girlfriend's son. Though he wasn't Derik's son, Derik felt an obligation to be his "dad" because the one he had was nowhere to be found. Caden would come over during the day on Saturdays while I was at work so he and Derik could do their faux father/son thing. This usually consisted of Derik having a moderate to severe hangover, and them watching movies or occasionally doing some sort of activity. Performing a noble duty had evolved into picking up his ex's kid and planting him in front of the TV. It seemed a little pointless to me, to not really be present or interested in his life, but just to have him around. I was convinced Derik continued this because he liked wearing the 'Good Guy' badge, not because he was truly invested in setting an example and guiding this kid, at least not anymore.

That morning we had our normal words about the situation, and I couldn't wait to get to work, "normal words" meaning I was in a bad mood due to the fact that deep down I knew that this situation would not end and that I would have to remove myself from it. The words involved me being distant and Derik trying to convince me that I needed to accept this situation. And I had, for a while. But now, I no longer wanted to be on this journey with Derik's ex-girlfriend's baggage. To a point I had known what I was getting myself into, but I had figured that since Caden wasn't his biological son, everyone would eventually move forward. I had been mistaken.

I remember I was wearing a red and silver tank top under a green dress that tied in the back. I wore red round toe platforms and a few gold necklaces. My hair was up in a ratty bun that was secured with a green headband. I had not washed it since I returned from Vegas. I was that run down. I wore silver dangle earrings.

I got to work and had brought my lunch: a pot pie. I had grocery shopped the night before when I had talked to my dad and we spoke about how he was now on a diet as directed by his doctor. He had been eating a lot of fish and salad. I told him I liked to make a salad with tuna, celery, lettuce, feta and capers.

"Don't forget the capers!" I had said.

"I think I still have some in the fridge," he said. He said he was going to have a beer after work. I told him to have fun and to call me tomorrow. We had planned to go to lunch that upcoming Monday at a burger joint near my house. I was excited to have lunch with my dad; just him and me. I could tell he was on the up-and up after the break up and it was actually refreshing to hear him in a somewhat normal state.

My pot pie was less than appetizing. It was bland and slightly stale. This disappointed me because I was really looking forward to it. I don't even eat pot pies, but for some reason it sounded really comforting, as I was on day five of a lingering hangover that just wouldn't quit.

It was around 11 a.m., and my dad hadn't called yet. He usually called on Saturdays when I was at work because he was at work, too. I thought this was a little strange, but I continued eating my lackluster pot pie and figured he was busy at work. He often got annoyed if we called him at work, so I let it be. I was counting down to my last clients.

The day had gone on and I was finishing up my second to last client. We were shooting the shit as usual. Laura is one of the nicest people I know. I feel as she knows me pretty well and that we are on the same page when it comes to being driven with our careers. We can talk for hours, and she always loved what I did to her hair.

I was flat-ironing her hair when Trevor, one of our assistants, came over.

"What do you need me to do?" Trevor asked.

"What do you mean?" I asked, a little confused.

"Derik needs to talk to you. What do you need me to do?" He asked again. He sounded weird.

"Tell Derik I will call him back. I am almost done," I said.

"No. Derik is here and needs to talk to you." He took the flat iron from me. Then I saw Melissa walking up front with my purse and jacket.

"Andi, Derik needs to talk to you. He is here." Trevor's eyes pierced into mine as he said this. This worried me. The first thought that went through my mind was that my house burned down...or something else bad had happened to my house.

I walked up to the front of the salon and saw Derik with a police officer and another woman. I knew it was a woman from Civilian's Aid. Our uncle had worked for them, and I knew right away. I knew whatever they had to tell me was important, but I had figured someone's house had burned down. Derik grabbed me by the hand. His hand was clammy and he was stark white and shaky. In the three years we'd been together at this point, I'd never seen him look like this. I was a little taken a back.

"I have some bad news," he said as lead me by the hand and out of the salon into the lobby.

(To Be Continued)

A Day in The Life

Our industry is nothing but glamorous. Well, salon life is far from the glamour portrayed in the fashion magazines, red carpet, and television shows. The reality of a hairdresser is quite the opposite of what is seen in "reality" shows. We work our asses off, standing on our feet for hours, perching over our clients, banging out quality work, laughing, and immersing ourselves in our own creative juices to get the job done, and in most cases dispensing therapy at no extra cost, all the while permanently crippling our bodies; morphing into hunch-backed vixens with feet, neck, back and wrist issues. And we do it all with a smile—and on a time crunch. I'm not complaining by any stretch; hell, I feel blessed to have lasted sixteen years and counting in the business. Hairdressers generally love what we do and love (most) of our clients. Our chosen field requires us to get up every day, look stylish—or at least we *should* look stylish— and make people feel and look amazing.

This industry is not for the weak and delicate. You have to be tough and learn early on to be criticized by clients and peers alike. It's hard, but Jesus, it gives you strength you didn't know you had. If you can handle constant judgment and criticism of your work, then you need to give yourself the credit you well deserve. We aren't in a field where we can have an "off" day and zone out in front of a computer and not talk to anyone if we are fighting with our significant other, reeling from a recent death in the family, having financial issues, hung-over, feeling sick, angry over a fender bender on the way to work, fighting with dramatic family members, or just having a bad fucking day.

In fact, it's quite the opposite. When our clients come to see us, it is expected that we be "on," regardless of the day we're having. It is what we do. People seek hairdressers not only for our skill in our craft, but also with the hope that later we become people that clients can confide in, vent to, and be entertained by. We have lives that bored housewives live vicariously through and probably envy. I'm sure each of us has one or two male clients that have sexually fantasized about us no less than a few times. We are constantly on our toes; our work being judged every 45 minutes. Our day is full of constant change in style and energy and conversation, and yet, once in a while during a blow-dry, I look around and think to myself: "Has it been this long, already?" Suddenly my career feels so monotonous and I feel the time on the clock crawl. I look around at my fellow ladies having cheerful conversations, putting up with their clients' bratty and misbehaved two-year-old (who I am secretly wanting to drop kick or at the very least duct tape its mouth and give it a tranquilizer), sweeping hair, answering phones and accommodating the rude and unreasonable; and I am grateful that the client in my chair is a long-time client and loyal woman that makes me laugh and makes me love what I do. We exchange a funny inside joke as I put the final touches on her cut and style and I walk her up to the desk so she can check out and re-schedule her next appointment. She is a generous tipper.

I head to the back room after checking out my client. This is supposed to be a place for our solace. Unfortunately, every back room I have ever experienced has offered little to no privacy from our clients. We would all love a little more privacy so we can have a place to just chill out, but I have learned to work around it, and my biggest concern is often what the client may over-hear while walking by to get to the restroom.

Despite our prefect appearances and professional demeanors, hairdressers are far more vulgar and gross than you think. We talk about things that probably only porn stars, drug addicts and career drunks are familiar with, and we cuss non-stop. To say we cuss like truck drivers is an understatement. 'Fuck' comes out of my mouth no less than 500 times a day, and 'Goddamn it' is a close runner up.

Hairdressers, or at least the ones I have worked with, have a real knack for turning innocent lunch table talk into something grotesque and perverse.

"Did you tell Mom?"

I was eighteen at the time, and my felon boyfriend
Rico was twenty-six. I was still living with my dad
in the Westside, and was working full time as a
hairdresser at a well-known salon chain called
Salon 35. I was doing pretty well. I was beginning
to build a clientele at a young age, and was excelling
in all of my classes that were mandatory at the
academy owned by the salon chain. It was like I
lived a double life. I worked at a high-end salon
with established hairdressers who seemingly had
their shit together and lived normal lives. Lives
filled with kids, husbands, mellow weekends. I was
living with my dad, as was my twenty-six-year-old
former cocaine-dealing, felon boyfriend who also
happened to be a cheating, abusive, waste of skin. I
was too worn down by the relationship, and
honestly quite ashamed. I didn't know enough at
the time of how get out of it. Coming to work with
a black eye made my colleagues aware of what I
was dealing with in my personal life, but, like all

abusers, Rico made me feel like I deserved it. I was manipulated into staying with him. He held my past full of sexual trauma and the textbook aftermath that comes along with it over my head, making me believe that no one would love or want damaged goods like myself. This kept me with him for five years off and on. *Who would want me?*

My friend and coworker, Alicia, had a friend that I resembled. Her name was Malia. She was Middle Eastern. I'm always mistaken for Middle Eastern, even though I don't have a drop of Middle Eastern blood. Alicia was always out partying (as was my abusive boyfriend and my dad). I felt left out of the loop, so Alicia suggested I get an ID from Malia and join the party. I was ecstatic. The last time I had a fake ID I was sixteen and I had my cousin Shannon's. That was back when there were things to do at eighteen like go to a club called The Player's Den where we'd dance the night away to hip hop and RnB. I'd later go to the Player's Den with my dad, his girlfriend, and Rico. This is what my life looked like: underage clubbing and drinking with my dad and felon boyfriend who was closer to thirty than twenty. I was barely old enough to buy the cigarettes I smoked.

I had only been using Malia's ID for a little while. I'd been getting into the newly opened The Haven nightclub with Rico and our group of friends, whom were mostly drug dealers that were running from the law, or on probation. The Haven nightclub was the place to be. The owners took an old, abandoned warehouse, and transformed it into a nightclub. It was one of the best clubs of that era that the city had seen. We even went there after my Alternative High School graduation. You know, because that's what you do after you graduate from Alternative High School…you go to the club. At least that's what I did. Most people go out for cake and pizza. We went to a nightclub.

The manager of the salon was turning twenty-one. The spot to be at the time was a club called Sky.

Yes, I had been there too with some of the other salon girls. Katie, our manager, had been looking forward to her birthday for quite some time. I was younger than she and was going out far more than she was. She was a little jealous, but that was all smoothed over by her being able to occasionally buy blow from a connection of Rico's.

As her birthday approached, something told me that I shouldn't go. It was a Monday, and I usually went to Sky with the same girls on the weekends because they knew the door guys and it was a safer bet I'd get in without getting sweated. Katie's birthday fell on a Monday, and we all planned to go out. It already sounded horrible, as Monday isn't a fun night to go out on (at least then it wasn't). I just had this feeling that I should stay home, plus I had to work on Tuesday, and I didn't want to be tired. At eighteen, I was already a seasoned veteran of the club scene and knew what it looked and felt like to go out on a school night. In the following years, I would ignore this internal voice, and daily hangovers would become my norm. At that time, I wasn't as tuned into my intuition as I am now. My gut was basically yelling at me not to go that night. But, I succumbed to peer pressure and went anyway.

It was a night in January and Rico and I were getting ready at my dad's house. I wanted to look cute and was quite proud of the fact that I was an up-and-coming hairdresser, so I wanted to look the part. I even remember telling Rico that I just wasn't in the mood. Surprisingly, he wasn't either. But, we had said we'd go, so go we did.

I remember feeling an energy when I walked up to the door of Sky, like I didn't belong there. I should have listened to that. But, I didn't.

"Can I see your ID?" the bouncer asked.

I pulled out my ID. He wasn't the usual bouncer I remembered from the other times I had been there.

He looked at the ID, then looked at me. Then looked at the ID, then looked at me again.

"What's your birth date?" he asked.

"June 17th, 1974." I had this memorized just in case. I wanted to be prepared should this question ever come up. I should have just walked away right then, but I'm stubborn, and I didn't want to lose.

"Ma'am, step aside please." The bouncer had me move to the side. There stood a cop. He was giving me an out, but I just listened to him, and looked back at Rico. It was like he knew what was going to happen.

"Sign your name on this." The bouncer wanted to see if I could sign the signature that was on the ID correctly. I got really nervous but assured myself that they most certainly would let me into the club and I'd dance the night away, even if it was a Monday.

I signed on the yellow pad three times like they asked me to, and the next thing I knew, two very large cops had me in handcuffs.

"You have the right to remain silent, everything you say can and will be used against you in a court of law," one of the large cops said.

"Those handcuffs fucking hurt," I snarked. And they did. Did they *really* need to tighten those fuckers to the point of them almost cutting off my circulation to my tiny wrists? For fuck's sake, I only weighed around 110.

"Ma'am, be quiet." I looked back at Rico, and he said he'd go to my dad's. The cop grabbed me roughly by the arm and equally as roughly sat me down on a hard bench. So hard that he ripped a hole in my new designer suede coat I had gotten for Christmas. I was pissed. I wasn't a huge threat, and Jesus Christ, I was only 5'1. What the fuck could I do!? I hadn't resisted arrest, and they were being unnecessarily rough. As soon as I was cuffed, the cops laughed amongst themselves as they told stories of other detainees they'd picked up that night.

"This is why people kill you mother fuckers!" I yelled to the arresting officer. I figured, what the fuck? I'm in custody. I might as well tell these fuckers how I and a lot of other people felt. A few weeks earlier, a local cop had been shot while on a call. As you can imagine, it was a controversial subject, and there was a lot of tension between civilians and law enforcement. Cops in the city were on high defense. But fuck these guys. I was getting arrested for a fake ID, and you have to be that rough with a 5'1 eighteen-year-old!? They had searched my purse and found nothing.

"Ma'am, we're going to have to ask you to be quiet," the cop snarked and laughed, and I was more pissed. I was fucking going to jail, and I had a full day of clients tomorrow. How the FUCK would I swing this one?

The advantage of having a felon for a boyfriend that was on probation for being involved in the fourth biggest cocaine bust in the state's history, is that you know exactly how this shit works. I knew I'd be booked, I knew once I was booked, (whenever that would be), that my bail would then be posted. I also knew at that time I'd be able to make my phone call, and hopefully someone had already posted my bail and I'd be released in the morning.

Once I was cuffed and read my rights, I was thrown in the paddy wagon. The paddy wagon is a windowless van with metal seats and two cops in the front. As I was placed into the paddy wagon, I took one look in and saw what appeared to be a couple of crack heads, a few homeless guys, one drunk lady that was on the verge of puking, and me. They don't tell you that once you're in the paddy wagon, you're basically on the equivalent of an airport shuttle to pick up all of the other detainees from their places of arrest. The cops take your shit once you're arrested and throw your possessions into a clear, plastic bag with your name and inmate number on it and throw it on the floor of the van. There I sat amongst my fellow detainees watching my designer purse and watch slide around the filthy floor of a police paddy wagon. I was too traumatized to be scared at this point.

A few stops later, we finally pulled up to the city jail. The cops had to unlock the cuffs that shackled my ankles together and let me out. The other detainees followed. We were led into a concrete room where they placed the females on one side of the room and the men on the other. The room was windowless and was lit by a few flickering fluorescent lights. There were more men than women being booked that night, one of which managed to pull out his penis and urinate on the floor right in front of everyone. He was, in every definition of the word, piss drunk. Petrified that the urine of a very drunk man would somehow touch my platform slides from my favorite high-end shoe store, I inched as far away from the stream of piss as I could without being noticed and yelled at.

The booking process went rather quickly. The females were led to the female wing by female officers who were much more well-mannered than our male counterparts who were being booked on the opposite side of the jail. All I could do was look around and hear something my mom had said to me once in regard to getting in trouble with the law: "Once you're in the system, you're always in the system." Was this true? Would I now lead a life of criminal activity? Lord knew I had done plenty of illegal things in my eighteen years of life; I had just never been caught. And to be caught with a fake ID!?

I entered the room where they take your mug shot. This process also went surprisingly fast. They call your name, you look at the camera, and 'click', there you go, off to the fingerprint area. The woman in front of me had this down. This was not her first time in the 'City', as it's referred to by regulars. I was a little impressed and saddened at the same time that she knew the process so well and seemed to be completely unbothered or affected by the fact that she was in jail. On a Monday. Again. For some reason she was holding up the fingerprint line. They repeatedly asked her to lay her thumbs and index fingers on the steel plate. Nothing was reading. Then the female booking officer figured it out. She was a prostitute and had too much lube on her hands to get a print reading. A few wipes of her hand on her teal green leggings, and she was finally able to get a clear print for booking. I was next in line, and much to my disappointment and slight horror, they didn't, in fact, wipe off the stainless steel plate for the next inmate. So, with the forceful assistance of the female officer, my finger was slapped right on top of the lube-saturated fingerprint reader. All I could think about is who this very young and very foreign prostitute was jacking off right before her arrest. Not only was she the prostitute holding up the fingerprint line, but she was my cellmate.

We were led to our cell and told to take off our bras. I was wearing a white mock-neck shirt, and they had taken my coat, so I was left feeling very exposed, because I was. I'm also incredibly self-conscious without a bra, so this in itself made me uneasy. Given my past of filled with sexual abuse and trauma, anything that made me feel slightly sexually vulnerable hit a part of me I'd prefer be internally hidden in my psyche.

Our cell was a small room with concrete walls and two bed-like tables that were attached to the walls.

There was a toilet and a sink. My cellmate went immediately to sleep, and I sat there wondering when my turn would come to make my call.

Jail cells are simultaneously repulsive and somber. You hear everything. You hear the loud, drunk, distorted voices of inmates. It's not only scary but also incredibly sad. I think it was more saddening to hear female voices. These were mothers, sisters, daughters, friends, or perhaps just lonely street drunks looking to get arrested on purpose so they'd have food to nurse their hangovers in the morning. The most unsettling thing I heard was a voice of a woman in a cell one down from us. You could tell she was yelling at the bottom of the cell door where there was a tiny crack of open space. Voices sounded so close yet so distant. Her seemingly whimpering voice sounded a little drunk, but also of someone who was in the state of suffering. I still vividly remember her saying, "I have AIDS. I need my meds. You can't deny me my meds. You have to call my doctor." At that moment it clicked that I never wanted to come back here. Not because this woman had AIDS—that didn't scare or threaten me—but because she wasn't being treated like a human. The officers were literally ignoring her. She called out repeatedly that she needed her meds. I had no reason to believe that she was lying. If you know anything about AIDS and the treatment of AIDS, you know that taking the prescribed meds exactly as directed is crucial. Certain meds were meant to be taken at certain times along with other meds, leaving little room for error. The precise consumption of these medications is crucial to the life of a person living with AIDS. The blatant disregard of the woman with AIDS infuriated and saddened me, and I vowed never to be a part of this legal system again. Once you're in custody, they don't give a fuck about you, your well-being, or if you live or die or take your meds. Yes, many of these people have done heinous things and are on their way to DOC, and those people deserve to be treated like the animals they are. However, a woman in custody with AIDS should have a right to the medicine that keeps her alive. Lesson learned—don't put yourself in a position to be treated like anything less than the human you are.

The time came for my phone call. I think by this time it was around 2:00 a.m., and I'd assumed and hoped that Rico had gone to my dad's for money and posted my bail, or one would hope given all the shit I'd done for him and all of his felony bullshit.

I was led out into the area where the phone calls are made. I picked up the receiver and dialed my dad's number. It rang a few times.

"Hello? Andrea?" my dad answered. He sounded sleepy yet not surprised or upset that his firstborn was sitting in the city jail on a Monday.

"Dad, did Rico come over?"

"Yeah, he said your bail was $110."

"Did you give him some money?" Rico had no money, and the two of us were living with my dad at the time. Rico was on probation for his felony drug charges, and when he was released from jail the year prior, we felt it would be a good idea for him to live with us under house arrest to keep him out of trouble. This would later become a huge mistake. Rico didn't have much money because of his extensive court fines, so I figured if he got money from my dad, I'd just pay my dad back.

"No, I don't have any money." These were my dad's favorite words. My dad's income went to alimony, child support, bills, beer, cigarettes, the occasional pot roast, and his weekends at the club with his unscrupulous girlfriend.

"Dad, how am I going to get bailed out?"

"I dunno. Rico said he was going to Luther's house to get some money." Luther was a drug dealer friend of Rico's. $110 to him was what he'd spend on lunch on a Wednesday. But to me, it was over a third of my paycheck.

"So, you didn't give him any money? I can't get out unless I get bailed out."

"Oh. Well, yeah, it sounded like he was going to get you bailed out." My dad was never a communicator, so this was about as far as the conversation was going to go.

"Did you tell mom?"

"Yeah, I told your mom."

"Fuck, dad! She's gonna be pissed. I need someone to call my work tomorrow. I have clients. Just tell them I'm sick or something."

"Alright, I'll tell your mom to call the shop."
Though my mom would be livid and disappointed

I'd spent the night in jail, she was the better option than my dad to call me into work.

"Don't forget. I can't just NOT go to work."

"I won't forget."

"Are you sure?"

"Yeah, I'll tell your mom to call the shop."

"Okay, well they're kicking me off the phone now."

"Okay. Bye." He hung up the phone as he coughed his smoker cough loudly into the receiver.

I was ushered back to the cell and wasn't one hundred percent confident that I'd ever be bailed out. Without bail, you have to go to court the next day, wait your turn, and hope the judge dismisses the charges and doesn't send you back to your cell.

My cellmate was still passed out. I sat on the floor reading whatever book they had in there. I felt like a complete piece of shit. The noise of the other inmates had died down a bit, but you could still hear people being booked and yelling profanities that didn't quite make sense. This obviously wasn't a place I belonged. I wasn't like these women with extensive track records and violent histories. I was a productive member of society with a blooming career in the beauty industry and impeccable talent. I was all of this with a felon boyfriend that was eight years older than me, and we resided in my dad's basement because he was on house arrest for violating probation for his felony arrest immediately following his involvement in the fourth biggest cocaine bust in the state's history. This would not be the only time in my career where I lived a double life of sorts. I should add that he was a mentally and physically abusive cheater.

"Breakfast!" the officer yelled, and our cell door slid open with a thunderous, mechanical boom. I followed my cellmate down to the population cafeteria. We grabbed our trays of food and sat down on one of the metal benches attached to the metal tables.

I looked down, and much to my displeasure, I saw two pieces of white bread, a boiled egg, grits, and a miniscule carton of 2% milk. I ate my white bread. I wouldn't touch the rest of that shit. The lady across from me didn't remember being arrested, and was still a little drunk. She asked me if she could have my boiled egg. I slid my tray to her, and she stuffed the egg down her shirt. Most of these women had been here before, and a few of them knew each other and were talking. It wasn't clear if they knew each other from their numerous trips to jail, or if they were homegirls outside of jail. It didn't matter. I just wanted the fuck out of there.

Breakfast was quick: twenty minutes, maybe. Back to our cells we went, and I peed in the open-air toilet. As predicted, my cellmate went immediately back to sleep. How could she sleep? I was actually pretty thankful she did. Imagine if I'd been locked up with one of those crazy drunk ladies talking my ear off through vomit breath. I'd take the petite, foreign prostitute with what appeared to be narcolepsy any day.

I tried to sleep and rest. Time in jail goes by at an excruciatingly slow rate. There are no clocks, and my watch was thrown in the plastic bag with the rest of my belongings, so I had no idea what time it was. I did see some pale sunlight trying to seep through the tiny, fogged glass window in our cell. This would mean it was around 7:00 a.m., and if Rico did in fact post my bail soon after my arrest, I would be out around 8. I sat there with anxiety and boredom.

At that moment, I wondered why habitual criminals did what they did. Besides the obvious habit of making bad decisions and being products of fucked up environments, what caused them to be repeat offenders? The boredom alone in a jail cell would drive anyone to insanity. Literally. What the fuck do you do but go inside the depths of your own head over and over again, and then one or two more times? The constant thinking and the noise and the cellmates was horrible. It was grotesque and a world that you can only know if you've been to jail. It's indescribable, really. Grey, loud, sterile, all lit up by fluorescent lighting which barely managed to showcase how archaic and dower the inside of a jail really is.

"Hunt, Andrea!" an officer called out.

"About fucking time," I said ever so softly under my breath. I didn't want to piss off the guards. One thing I learned through all of Rico's bullshit was you have to play the game or you can monumentally fuck yourself. Just shut the fuck up, do what you're told, and shit won't get worse.

My cell door opened, and an officer was standing there with my things. I quickly put on my coat, and they led me to the phone. I called Rico at my dad's house, and he drove my jeep to come get me.

I was standing outside of the jail waiting for him to come get me. It was a grey, cloudy morning, and I felt like I had completely fucked up my life. I looked down at the ticket I was issued, and I had to return to court in about a month to do god knows what.

Rico arrived, and I got in the car and we went home. I showered, cried, ate, and went to sleep— with my bra on.

Can I Help You?

The success or demise of a salon can fall on the shoulders of the front desk staff, or more accurately, who the person in charge of hiring the front staff may be. If a salon owner decides to hire a receptionist who isn't well put together, or friendly, or can multi task, you can very well be shooting yourself in the foot. Most receptionists that I have worked with are all the same. They want to work in a salon; they think it will be relatively easy and want part time hours to either finish school or work their second job. Most of the gals that have booked my appointments, dealt with client phone calls—good and bad, pushy and nice—have been fairly normal, but all seem to get jaded after a while. Catering to clients on a daily basis from morning till night can have its adverse effects. This is probably due to the fact that they take all of the shit that our clients give them but won't give to us and are forced to do it with a smile and grace, or at least most of them.

I had just figured out that The Main Hotel and Spa was pretty much screwing me over. Not pretty much actually: they *were* screwing me over. I had to get out before I lost any more clients that I had carefully brought over from Salon 35, which was my first gig. I had learned that on my days off, the receptionists were telling my clients that were calling for me that I was either too busy or unavailable. They were then scheduling them with other stylists on days that I wasn't there. The Main Hotel and Spa had seen me and my steady book of clients as an opportunity to feed their existing stylists and keep money in their pocket while giving me the runaround and telling me I had to revert to being an assistant. My coworker, Annika, had suggested I go over to Chic salon, which was a half block away. Chic was born out of the recent walkout at The Main. The former manager, Deborah Nichols, was now the owner, as was

Eddy, or he—at least—would like to think he was. I decided to go over there one day and apply for any job they had. I had rent to pay and I had seventeen dollars in my bank account. I was fucked.

I walked over to Chic, and walked in the door. Two women are sitting at the desk, neither one of them looking like they work at a high-end salon in downtown. One of them looks like she would be a high school gym teacher, the other a jaded librarian, not because librarians are typically jaded, but because she was frumpy and super grouchy. It seemed like with every passing second she was more and more put off by humanity. I am wondering if I am indeed in the right place. Esthetically, it looked like the salon Annika had described, but the vibe at the front desk was far from warm and friendly. They sent out a vibe that they were constantly being put off by anyone who approached them for anything, which was ironic seeing how their job was to accommodate clients and their needs.

Nothing peeves me more than when I walk into an establishment and the receptionist/hostess/clerk does not acknowledge me. This is what happened when I walked into Chic.

Since I was not greeted by either one of the women, I had to get this thing going myself.

"Hi. I was wondering if the owner is available?" I ask.

"And who are you?" a mouth void of the ability to smile asks rudely…very rudely. I am thinking of aborting my mission if this is how this salon operates. But, I am desperate and have to pay the bills.

"My name is Andrea Hunt. Annika sent me to talk to either Deborah or Bridget. I work at The Main."

I wasn't nervous, per se, but I didn't feel welcome in the least bit.

"I'm Bridget. I'm the manager. What can I help you with?" She was a tad warmer than the other one, but I could immediately tell she had an abrasive side. Her abrasiveness would later lend itself to quick and dry humor, which meant that she and I became friends for years to come.

"I was wondering if you guys are hiring. I work at The Main and Annika has told me a lot about you guys," I said.

"Oh nice. Annika. Yes, she is our friend. I think we are hiring for an assistant position. Why don't you fill out an application and I will grab Deborah and you can talk to her," Bridget said. She'd ever-so-slightly changed her disgruntled tune.

I could tell she was going to talk about me to Deborah in a gossipy way. But, whatever. She brought out an application, and as I filled it out, I noticed that the jaded librarian was very distant and short with each client. Maybe this *is* how they do things. Not only did she not fit the profile of a receptionist in a downtown salon, but she was also rude.

As I finished filling out the application, Deborah came out and introduced herself. She also did not look the part, but came across as very professional and no nonsense. I felt good about this. As she looked at my application, she started talking to me about her history as a manager and now owner. Deborah was very impressed with all of the experience I had accumulated over my then three-year career. She hired me on the spot, but only as an assistant until there was room for me to go on the floor full time. She said I could take clients on Saturdays. This would allow me to accommodate what clientele I had left from the disaster at The Main and to start to re-build. I was ecstatic. I was to start in one week. I immediately quit The Main, and got ready for my new gig.

Starting at Chic wasn't exactly a warm-welcome experience. I must admit, after being a full time stylist for the last few years, it was tough to go back to assisting. But, it paid an hourly wage and that is exactly what I needed, even if it was five dollars an hour (I'd also soon land a side job dancing on a cube on Friday and Saturday nights at a nightclub for fifty dollars and free drinks). I remember wondering on my first day if the two aloof women would grow any nicer. I remember Sandy being the only one who was engaging and nice to me. From the get, you could tell that these people had a history and were cliquey. The other assistant, Aleasha, was covered in tattoos and the skinniest thing I have ever seen. She was cool. We clicked right away over our love of house music, cigarettes, and tattoos.

I started on a Saturday, so it was busy. I observed the mood and behavior of the receptionist, Christa, and of the manager, Bridget. They both still seemed putout at the front desk. Bridget seemed to have a deeper history with a few of the employees/clients, and she and Eddy often laughed at their own jokes. Christa always seemed to have a stuffed nose and was constantly blowing it. And sneezing. Always. She literally could not complete a sentence without sneezing. Her nose was permanently red, and she sounded congested around the clock. *What was she allergic to?* I'd often wonder.

As my first weeks at Chic went on, Christa turned slightly warmer. I began to figure out that she was kind of a depressed person and that came out at work. All around, she was just not that happy. Her family was a bit strange: like a very small town mentality—almost like they'd never been out of their tiny town though they actually lived right outside of the city. There was something just not quite right with these people. I believe that her sister, her sister's husband, and their small child lived with Christa's parents in a small house. Christa did not come from money and lived in a room she rented from an elderly couple near one of the city's oldest parks. She walked to work every day to save money on parking. After getting to know her better, she started to be a little more open and slightly nicer to me. I remember her mentioning that she would eat because she was depressed, and often times lonely. I felt bad for her. I felt bad that she didn't come from much yet had hopes of going to school to become a teacher, and I felt bad that she had two teeth missing. Things like acne, obesity, and bad teeth break my heart. In my opinion, if you have a child with any of the above, it is your responsibility as a parent to correct it. I felt bad that she had reached her mid-twenties missing two teeth. It clearly made her sad, insecure, and uncomfortable with herself.

Christa was the type of person who always had something wrong with her, like her glasses that needed to be fixed or her constant allergies. I mean *constant* around-the-clock nose-blowing and nasal congestion. She fascinated me with how she always brought a peanut butter and jelly sandwich on white bread to work every day for lunch. She also always had apples in some sort of watered-down, creamy sauce. I asked her one day what it was. She said she sliced up apples and put milk over them and she liked how it tasted after they sat for a few hours They turned into that watery apple snack. As I got to know her, I actually learned she would talk your ear off about absolutely nothing. She would just talk and talk. I think she was put on anti-depressants at one point. This is when the chattiness increased. I also think she was very lonely and sought company with anyone who would talk to her.

After about three years at Chic, I felt my time there had run its course. I wasn't alone in my urge to move on. Many of the original employees were sick of Bridget and her alleged controlling ways and Deborah and her...well...her. I had never really had serious issues with either one of them. In fact, I clicked with both of them and felt we had a mutual respect for each other.

Marc, a sophisticated gay man, had moved here from New Hampshire and started over. He owned a high-end salon in New Hampshire and was a master of his craft. He was a true artist and professional. Always impeccably dressed, he came to work and wowed me with his effortless ability to connect with his clients and to give some of the best haircuts I'd ever see in my career.

Lo and behold, after a year of being micromanaged and ordered around by our superiors at Chic, Marc opened up his own salon. Sandy, Vanessa, Kris, and I decided to jump ship.

Honestly, for me the move was not about the management, but about the surroundings. Chic was a full-on party crew and until I met Eddy and Desiree and a few of the others, I pretty much had my drinking in check. Cocaine became a huge issue for me. Unbeknownst to all of my friends who worked there, I had gone through some outpatient treatment for substance abuse. At the time, I knew I needed help, but I wasn't quite ready to let go of the party. I thought if I left, got away from my surroundings, I could maybe get my act together. So, my departure from Chic wasn't about management or my dislike of the products. It was about getting away from the partying and toxic lifestyle that so many of the stylists shared, and hopefully pull myself together a little bit. Unlike my peers who could control their recreational partying, I could not. I had a problem. I was an addict. I have never shared that period of my life before.

Dennis was Marc's partner. When I asked who was going to be working our front desk, Marc said that

Dennis' sister would do it. I thought that like birds of a feather…. She *must* be fabulous and refined and put together like Dennis. Not a day went by when Dennis wasn't decked out in head-to-toe designer brands. He had impeccable taste in fashion, art, food, and culture. Both he and Marc did. Much to my surprise, Dennis' sister, Samantha, was not at all what I expected. She didn't have the refined taste and etiquette that Dennis possessed. Not even close. Did they have the same parents? The only way I could describe her is to say that she was reminiscent of the women that would go on talk shows in the late 80s and early 90s, and because they were dating or married to a Mexican man or a cholo, they too thought they were of that heritage. But both Dennis and Samantha were as white as they come.

On our first day at Marc Thomas Salon, named after Marc himself, I was really excited to start anew. Marc had ensured me that we'd have a much more laid back atmosphere at his salon and that we'd be a lot more creative and focused on fashion shows and editorial work. I loved the sound of all of this. I needed a distraction from my addiction issues.

I walked in the door in my latest euro-designer outfit, and much to my alarm, Samantha was at the desk, snapping her gum, dressed in an ankle-length skirt, a sweatshirt, and a pair of open-toed shoes that accentuated the fact that she'd not seen a pedicure in maybe forever. She had long, acrylic nails that were like the ones I had in beauty school in 1995. They protruded at least an inch from the tip of her finger—at least. They were a shade of pink that was so bright, it was blinding, and three of them were missing. Her hair was still wet from her shower, and she had failed to wipe off yesterday's makeup. I was in disbelief. Marc had sunk a fortune into the space. There was nothing that wasn't exactly perfect and fashionable, even down to our overpriced glasses we used to serve water to our clients. Yet this was our receptionist/salon manager?

I greeted her. "Hi, I'm Andi."

"Samantha." More snaps of her spearmint gum. The one thing that makes me homicidal is the sound of someone smacking and snapping their gum like they're a chola on meth. She actually might have been a chola on meth. But she's white. And, since her married last name was more Mexican than my white last name, I guess she considered herself to be of Mexican decent.

Samantha was never in a good mood, mostly because she was fighting with her husband Manuel. Manuel never came around the salon. All we knew about him was that he and Samantha had three kids together, and they lived in a small apartment in the suburbs somewhere. He was an aspiring tattoo artist—in and out of work—and Samantha was the breadwinner. It was sad and infuriating at the same time. His shitty choices and laziness always caused her bad moods.

The thing about a front desk person that's in a bad mood is this: it sets the tone for the whole day. If the receptionist comes to work in a bad mood, they take it out on the stylists because they can't take it out on the clients, even though they'd like to. If the receptionist is fighting with her significant other, is running late, is on her period, or is dealing with whatever else is causing her sour mood, the day can be a living hell. Because of this-or-that, the receptionist will feel put out when asked to do their job. Stylists won't be alerted when their clients arrive, and phone calls are handled in a rude, abrupt manner, and in the case of Samantha's bad moods, the gum-snapping and smacking will be intensified.

I think the only reason I made it through my few years at Marc Thomas Salon was because I had more important things to worry about—like how I was going to conceal my hangover and runny nose from doing too much blow the night before. Although it was my intention to get away from all the partying, you can't outrun your addictions, not unless you face them and the root cause of them head on. I was still in my early to mid-twenties, and I was showing no signs of slowing down my drug and alcohol habits. Because of this constant cycle of acting like I wasn't still high on coke from the night before, or that I was on the edge of puking, I had little time or attention to pay to Samantha or her bad moods.

Samantha did come around, eventually. She divorced her loser husband and finished school. Marc had given her a makeover per our request. The front desk person is the primary representative of the salon and the first person clients see. Coming to work with wet hair wasn't exactly setting the beauty standard high, so we saw to it that Marc cut and colored her hair on a regular basis. I even chipped in by showing her some makeup techniques. She was apprehensive at first. She felt like she was bothering us, and as moody as she could be, she insisted on tipping us, which was completely unnecessary. She didn't quite know how to say it, but she was profoundly grateful. It was almost like she so badly wanted to be the pretty girl with the trendy hair and cute clothes, but her own insecurities and self-doubt got in her way. Plus, a verbally abusive husband didn't help matters.

Something remarkable happens when we, as beauty industry service providers, use our talents to help someone who doesn't do their hair, let alone experiment with color and cut trends. An esthetic and psychological transformation takes place. The walls of insecurity and anger come down. That's exactly what happened to Samantha. All it took was one haircut, an auburn brown shade of hair color, a new lip color, and an eyebrow shaping, and her new-found confidence emanated from her like rays from the sun. She transformed from a grouchy, frumpy woman with an identity crisis, to a jovial, confident, trendy woman with a new-found look on life, and more importantly, herself. Samantha was working and acting in ways she never thought possible. It was quite fun to watch...and rewarding.

Witnessing this sort of metamorphosis on a daily basis is the reason we do what we do. The transformation of Samantha was the first of many learning experiences in my career as to what hairdressers are capable of achieving. What we do is very psychological. What we look like on the outside is often times very indicative of what is going on inside. In Samantha's case, her new outer-appearance had trickled inside of her somewhere deep and planted the seeds of self-confidence. Samantha's seeds continued to grow and bloom. And to think, it all started with a haircut.

Table 10

Any hairdresser that says they go to New York to learn is full of shit. It is a full-on party from the time you land; actually, I take that back. It's a full-on party from the time you get to the airport and throw back some airport wine. Wait, I take that back too. It is a full-on party the second you step out of the salon knowing you are heading to NYC for "education." Before you even get to the airport, you down a couple of martinis with your girls and get nice and tuned the fuck up. The party continues in the car or cab on your way to the airport and takes a brief break when you are checking in. Then you head straight to the bar before going to the gate. When you board, you immediately order a bottle of airplane wine…and maybe a second. Then, perhaps you take a small nap to gear yourself up for the non-stop debauchery that will consume you and your girls for the next three days.

The first time I went to New York for a hair show to "learn and become inspired" was everything I thought it would be. I went with Gwen. A petite woman, Gwen was covered in tattoos and had jet-black hair that was cut into what we hairdressers refer to as a Chanel bob. At the last minute, one of our co-workers decided to come along for the ride. Holly was in her fifties, kind of rustic and in my opinion a little on the socially awkward side. After this trip, she proved to be completely and utterly socially awkward.

Travel day had arrived, and we get off of work and headed to the bar to have some drinks before catching our red eye. I have two extra-dirty vodka martinis. Gwen has the same. Oh, and of course we have to go pick up Holly because she has not packed yet and is doing so while we imbibe. I'm already annoyed. How can you not be packed for a trip that you've known about for over a month?

I should mention I am doing a sort of long-distance dating thing with a gentleman who is friends with the boyfriend of a co-worker. He is a waiter. Actually he calls and still does call himself an actor who is always working on a screenplay. Conveniently for me/us, he works at the hot spot for sushi and all things Japanese and celebrity in New York City. They are booked months in advance, even for the likes of Oscar-winning actresses and supermodels. and Giselle, unless, of course one of the waiters/actors is trying to fuck you and has been trying for a good year now. At any rate, I love sushi, so I have my long-distance friend make a reservation for Holly, Gwen, and me. Some friends were in the city a few months prior and had dinner there as well. A celebrity studded sushi joint sounded good to me. Not only was he to make a reservation for us, but he was going to show us the city. Well, show me the city—in the hope of getting to fuck me.

We pick up Holly and head to the airport, where we order more drinks at the only airport restaurant that is still open. Like clockwork, I'm experiencing an alcohol-induced cigarette craving. My friend Holly had a pack of cigarettes. Thank God. But wait: we are in the terminal. What to do? Smoke in the bathroom of course. So we go smoke in the airport bathroom. The six-month anniversary of the September 11 terrorist attacks on the World Trade Center is less than a week away, and here we are: smoking in the airport bathroom. Who the fuck cares about heightened security at the airport? I am hammered and simply must have a cigarette. This is non-negotiable. So, we successfully finish our bathroom smoke, and meet Gwen in the terminal. With slight embarrassment and a high level of concern, she asks: "What the fuck are you doing?"

"We went to smoke a cigarette." I slur.

"You fucking idiots. If we get kicked out of here, I'm going to be fucking pissed." Gwen is a mother of two, and the disciplinarian in her is now taking effect on Holly and me.

"Well, we board the plane soon, and I need to smoke before that." I walk off with a slight stumble with my arm wrapped around Holly, and we find a telephone booth.

Holly and I light up one of her Camel Lights. No one notices the smoke or the smell during this very high-security time in our airports. But, we are both drunk and need a cigarette, so we smoked again…in the airport…nearly six months after 911. Not one person noticed. Not one. Not a security guard, a janitor, a patron. Not one.

Finally, we board and I immediately pass out. That was the best sleep I had had in a long while, probably because I was nearly to the stage of blackout drunk, and didn't have my usual amount of cocaine in my system to keep me up all night. I slept well, but actually sitting down in my seat is something I don't even remember.

"Wake up!!" Gwen asserts through gritted teeth. It took a few minutes, but I finally woke up as a result of her shaking me. I open my eyes, and it registers where I am. I immediately smell a foul odor on the plane, like morning breath, ketchup, and feet.

We get to our hotel all the way in mid-town. Being the NYC virgin I was, I was very excited to see Times Square until I actually got there. I guess that is to be expected when it is your first time. Its grotesque amount of tourists, energy waste, and chain restaurants make it underwhelming and disappointing.

We check in to the hotel and immediately head to the "restaurant" located in the lobby. I order a plate of bacon. That was it: just a plate of bacon. How I didn't weigh four hundred pounds at that time is quite miraculous. I mean, I was a little softer, but with the amount of booze and fatty foods I lived on, you'd expect me to be gargantuan.

After I devoured my plate of bacon, we all go up to the room and nap. I need to pull it together before we meet up with Hugh. I can't be a hung-over, bacon-smelling mess. Jesus, help me.

We rally ourselves, and after we shower/sober up, we go shopping. We were to meet Hugh and his friend at his apartment in the East Village later that night. Lots of shopping and wandering later, we go back to the hotel and get ready.

Forgetting that the whole "purpose" of this trip was to go to the World Beauty Conference, we start on the wine again in the room. The WBC is a very large and exhausting hair show held every spring at the Convention Center. To my knowledge, the WBC is little more than an excuse to go to New York, party with your fellow hairdressers, and expense then deduct the whole thing on your taxes in the name of "education." That basically describes the mindset. But, it was my first time so I thought I would give it a shot. Gwen and I had signed up for a class the next day or the day after or whenever. It was a three-day show. As long as we made an appearance and showed our boss our ticket stub, it didn't really matter to us. I was here to party, drink, eat sushi, and be shown around town by an actor/waiter.

We meet Hugh at his 300-square-foot apartment. He somehow has managed to squeeze in a roommate. Hugh offers us a drink made from infused vodka. I couldn't tell you what it was infused with—strawberries maybe? Who knows? We drink our jungle juice and meet Hugh's friend Aaron at a restaurant called Brava. We all had wine and tapas. The night was off to a good start. Hugh and his friend were really fun and hilarious. I've got a soft spot in my heart, (and sometimes panties), for funny members of the opposite sex. Their endless stories about being waiters/actors residing in NYC and working at *the* restaurant of the moment made me want to move to New York. It also made me want to fuck Hugh. He was hot, funny, charming, and had washboard abs. Gwen and I are having a ball. Holly is being her socially awkward self, and asking random and irrelevant questions and I feel like she is out of place a bit. But I'm a bottle of wine deep, I'm in New York, and I'm having the time of my life.

We leave Brava to go to a bar called Linear. Apparently you have to be on a list of some sort to get in. Aaron proceeds to give the bouncer some bullshit story about how he is so-in-so's brother, friend, or cousin. I recall him making a phone call to someone in L.A. so they could talk to the bouncer and convince him to let us in. It was a lot of hoops to jump through, but the guys wanted to impress the gals. The phone call worked and we were in.

We were having fun dancing and drinking when we notice a middle-aged man dressed in a suit and tie dancing all by himself in this lounge. He was a little creepy, and far from graceful, so of course Holly liked him. The night carries on and Gwen and Holly leave. I crash with Hugh in his shipping crate/apartment. I have to get up somewhat early to get back the hotel and get ready for this education show or class or whatever I'm supposed to be attending. As I awake in Hug's bed, I'm a little euphoric from the wine, the making out, and the fact that I'm in NYC. I walk myself out of his building, and wait for a cab outside of the apartment and take it all in. I love it. I love the energy and grit and sounds and sights. I never want to leave.

I get back to the hotel, and we get ready, we go to the show for five minutes, and Gwen and I decide to jet. Holly says she will meet up with us in a bit. Holly is a woman who is completely unaware of her surroundings. She's also completely oblivious to how unaware of her surroundings she actually is. She is that woman in the mall that will just stop for no goddamn reason in front of you or walk slowly without purpose, just looking blankly into nothing. You want to punch her in the back of the head so she will either fall over so you can walk around her or so she'll move out of your way. Being the ADD people we are, Gwen and I have very little tolerance for this. We have better things to do than be bothered by Holly and these annoying fucking hairdressers that are trying to sell us everything from shampoo to shears to brightly colored hair extensions. So, naturally, we go shopping.

That evening Holly and Gwen do their own thing and Hugh and I are to hang out and do something. I meet him at a Thai restaurant named Kaffir. We eat then go grab coffee. The night was mellow and I feel grown-up, but I'm also twenty-three, and in New York for the first time. Knowing how I like to dance—and dance to hip hop in particular—Hugh has done his research on underground hip hop clubs in the city. We hit one more bar before we go to the hip hop club.

Being the only white, and I mean very white, guy…and being that he's wearing a fleece and drinking a micro-brew, Hugh stands out a bit. He is the only Caucasian in the nightclub. But it's okay. He's with me, and I'm a petite Latina with an ass. He's good. Of course he can't/doesn't/won't dance with me. No worries, I take it to the floor myself. Black men have always loved me, and tonight is no different. I continue dancing to Wu Tang and Nas with a rotund black man who is getting a kick out of the whole situation. He sees me go kiss Hugh in between songs and come back to the floor to dance. Hugh is making the most out of being so completely out of place. He's also drunker than shit.

The rest of the night is a blur for both of us. I end up at his crate/apartment again. I think *holy fucking headache* when I wake up. It feels as if my brain is completely devoid of liquids. My head is pounding, and if I don't get out of here soon, I'll probably puke in his bed. We both feel like shit. We both have pounding headaches and don't remember much of the night. He calls me a nut bag. This can only imply that I was completely and utterly out of control last night, but like I always said, if I don't remember, it didn't happen.

And today, of all the days on the trip, I have to attend a 90-minute class at WBC. Fuck me. No, don't fuck me. I might puke. I wander around his room, grabbing my clothes, and head downstairs. I hail a cab to the hotel. The smell of a NYC cab when you've got a hangover is the kiss of death. I pray I don't vomit. I also realize that I somehow managed to put my panties on backwards. This is an uncomfortable feeling when coupled with the dizzying impact of my dehydrated body.

I get to the hotel and get as ready as I can. I really need to pull it together, not for the class, but for the reservation we have tonight at Hugh's workplace. I can't go into the place looking like I do now. I'm the color of cigarette ashes, and my eyes are glossy with dark circles that only enhance how glossy they are.

Gwen and I go to class and I wear my sunglasses the whole time trying with intense effort not to puke on her or anyone else. The haircutting class was taught by a French stylist who I had never heard of. My sunglasses were never removed and covered up the fact that I was rolling my glazed-over eyes at his overly-detailed description of each and every strand of hair he cut. Looking back, I guess he had to elaborate because the model had maybe ten hairs, tops. What should have been a haircut that took fifteen minutes was dragged to ninety minutes. I actually have to give it to him: he was able to make something so basic and easy look like the haircut version of a Monet. Well done, Frenchie. Class finally ended, and it was a success. I managed to learn a little something and not vomit on Gwen or the mid-western hairdressers in front of us. Now to reward myself with more shopping.

The three of us head downtown, and Holly is getting on my nerves. She is walking too slow, taking forever to decide on anything, and having unnecessarily lengthy conversations with store clerks about absolutely nothing. Crossing the street with busy New York traffic proves especially challenging. All you have to do is walk. Don't stop in the middle of the fucking street and look around at the sky scrapers. Fucking walk. We end up in the Village and shop and wander. Gwen would love to throw Holly under a subway car at this point. Gwen and I decide we are going to get tattoos. Gwen got Chinese symbols on the top of each foot. Much to my own surprise, I made a very adult decision NOT to get a tattoo. Something in my vodka-marinated brain told me that this was not a good idea. And I actually listened.

Our dinner reservations are in two hours and we have to high-tail it back to the hotel and then back downtown to Tribeca. At this point we are on Canal Street so Holly can buy a knock-off handbag. I hate knockoffs. Hate. *Finally,* Holly decided on a few knockoffs and we got the hell out of there. Who knew picking out three of the most un-interesting knock-off purses would be like picking out a house you were about to purchase. Fuck, man.

We get to the hotel, down some wine while getting ready, and Holly begins to tell us about how her dowdy, middle-aged boyfriend ties her up and fucks her. She also mentioned something about a threesome and going down on some woman. I had quit paying attention. I had to focus on my eyeliner and hair. I really had to pull out all the stops with Hugh tonight after my episode last night…well, what I remembered of it. I couldn't allow myself to get sidetracked with Holly's tales of kinky sex with her ass-deficient boyfriend.

We get to the restaurant, and I am so excited for this food, for this entire experience. We're in a celebrity-studded restaurant, and my soon-to-be fuck buddy will be our waiter. We get seated and Hugh comes over and is green—green and hungover beyond belief. He's almost unrecognizable. He was literally the color of cinder and pea soup. He was eight years older than I, and last night he proved as much.

"Don't look now, but Cindy Crawford and Christy Turlington are right behind you," he says to me.

Gwen and I are sitting next to each other and Holly is across from us. Cindy and Christy and Gwen and I are back-to-back.

"Is that Cindy Crawford?!" Holly shouts/slurs.

"Dude, shut the fuck up. You are so loud," I say. Hugh had said not to make a big deal out of it, so we didn't. I am a total star fucker, but there was no need to make a fool out of myself. Again.

Holly carries on. She's to that point of drunkenness that she's no longer making sense and is slurring and mumbling. She goes to the bathroom. Annoyed and hungover, Hugh comes over to drop off our Hamachi jalapeno sashimi.

"Look what your girl did," he says. He shows me a collection of chopsticks and the river rocks from the fountain that are placed down his pants. Apparently, when Holly went to the bathroom, she took a detour to the waiter station and thought it would be cute to shove chopsticks and fountain river rocks down his pants.

"For fuck's sake. What the fuck?" As I am saying this, Holly comes around the corner and starts to chat up the table next to us. It is filled with two couples who are on a double date, and Holly sits her drunk self at their table and makes herself at home. At least she is out of our hair for the moment.

All too soon, she's back. We finish dinner and Hugh finishes his waiter/actor shift. The plan was to go to the well-known strip club Table 10. The four of us catch a cab. Hugh is in the front, and Holly, Gwen and I are in the back.

A friend had recommended Table 10 and wanted us to get her a t-shirt from there. I guess it was her favorite talk show host's titty bar of choice in the Big Apple, so she wanted to have a piece of memorabilia. I've never been one to turn away a lap dance, so why not?

We arrive at Table 10, all of us except Hugh are feeling pretty tipsy. Poor Hugh. We have been out every night till sunrise drinking like it's our job. It could be my job. It really should have been my job.

We sit down, and like a fat kid on a sandwich, a stripper approaches us immediately. Strippers love when women come to the club, and we were the only other women there aside from the strippers.

"Would you like a lap dance?" she says in the thickest Lawng Island accent ever.

"Yes, we would love one," I say.

So Gwen, Hugh, and I proceed to get a lap dance.

"You are so beauty-full! Oh my gawd!" the dancer says to me.

"Thank you!" I say. "What is your name?"

"My name? Babette!"

She is blabbing on and on and on, and then she raises her arms, crosses them in the air, bends at the elbow so her hands are on her side boob, and

clacks her boobs together. This makes us laugh.
Babette keeps talking about who-knows-what.
Hugh is ready to pass out from exhaustion. That is
what happens when you hang out with a twenty-
three-year-old for three days solid. Aside from
Babette, Table 10 was not what we thought it
would be. I was expecting beautiful topless
goddesses, and instead, there were strippers from
surrounding boroughs trying to make their rent,
along with bouncers in cheap suits.

Gwen and I decide we haven't had enough yet so
we decide to stay out longer. Hugh, exhausted,
goes home; Gwen and I go to a bar.

We end up at a bar near Times Square. I think.
Gwen and I had a great time just being dumb,
drunk, and loud. Our sushi dinner was fantastic
and all, but we were starving. So in true drunk
fashion, we stumble over to a fast food joint. It was
disgusting yet tasty at the time. We are hammered
and eating our chicken tenders and decide to call

our friends and co-workers Desiree and Eddy…for two reasons: we knew they would be up and we were going to tell them we were partying with the strippers from Table 10 and there would be potential for an orgy (gross, never). Eddy and Desiree were probably just drunk enough to believe our fabricated story, so we went with it. They relished in that shit. The crazier the better.

"Hello?" Desiree answers. Her voice sounds of cigarettes and whiskey.

"What are you doing?" I ask

"Nothing. Hanging out with Eddy. What are *you* guys doing?" she asks in a curious fashion. I knew she was hoping something scandalous would go down in New York.

"We are in a limo with the strippers from Table 10 and they just gave us some ecstasy," I say. Gwen is laughing as quietly as someone like her can. She's the very antithesis of quiet.

"WHAAAAAAAT??????? Oh my God, Eddy. Andi and Gwen are with the strippers from Table 10. They are taking pills. Oh my God, Andi. Where are you going? How many are there? Are they hot? How many drugs have you done...?" I can hear the jealousy in her voice. Gwen and I are chowing down on chicken tenders, and are drunk as fuck and having a pretty good laugh at this.

"I don't know where we're going. I think some after-hours club. We're on the list. Gwen and I. Half the staff of Table 10 is with us." I lie, dipping a handful of fries in barbeque sauce.

"Eddy," she says, trying to get his attention as I hear her pull a drag of a cigarette deep into her throat. "Eddy, they're going to an after-hours club. Them and the girls from Table 10." This doesn't excite him nearly as much as it does Desiree, and I can hear him turn up the stereo to drown her out. True to form, he blasts Janet Jackson. At this point, I just want to finish our little joke and eat the rest of my fries, and drink my orange drink.

"Hey, Desiree, I gotta go. One of them wants to kiss me or go down on me or something..." I press 'end' on my flip phone, and hang up. Gwen and I are laughing our asses off at the fact that having a stripper want to kiss you or go down on you is disgusting and that Desiree *totally* bought it.

Desiree blows up my phone the next morning and wants details.
My phone keeps ringing. I'm foggy in the head, and my stomach feels like it might explode right inside of my abdominal cavity.

"Hello?" I answer, searching the hotel room for a bottle of water or anything to help my tongue not feel like a piece of sandpaper.

"I want all the details." Desiree commands.

"Details about what?" I ask through a fucking pounding headache and increasing gastro-intestinal issues.

"About the girls from Table 10!" I am surprised she is one: awake and two: remembered any of that. I barely did.

"Dude, you believed me? Oh my God. We were totally joking. Oh yes, like I would ever let some stripper go down on me. Sick."

"Oh." She says. We hang up. There's no time for this. We are getting ready to go to Ground Zero, Then, Hugh is meeting me to hang out before we catch our flight.

The girls and I walk through town and hit a disturbing level of silence when we approach Ground Zero. There are fences completely covered with flags, pictures, clothes, posters, and flowers. For as loud as New York is, the silence at Ground Zero was deafening. The site was fenced–in, and parts of the debris were still smoking. It was astounding. Seeing all the FDNY and the hundreds of people gathered there in silence as many, many coroner trucks were hauling out the remains was an experience I cannot put into words. A woman carrying a beautiful bouquet of calla lilies approached the fence and wanted to lay her flowers there.

"Ma'am, you are going to have to back up; no one beyond this point." An officer tells her.

"I just want to lay these down," she says in a very thick New York accent.

"I am not going to tell you again: step back!" the officer says, in an even heavier New York accent.

"Well you know what? Go fuck ya self!" the woman shouts; throwing the officer the middle finger.

"No, you go fuck YA self!" the officer shouts

"No, YOU go fuck YA self!!!" she shouts back.

All of that pierces the dead silence of mourning.

We leave the site. The girls go to the hotel, and I meet up with Hugh. He takes me around the city and we have pizza and do all sorts of touristy this-and-that. Now the exhaustion settles in.

I meet with the girls and we head to La Guardia. As we are going through security, Holly gets pulled aside. The security guard runs her bag through the scanner a few times and pulls out a pair of hair-cutting shears that are splayed wide open. Gwen and I are very over being around her and head to the gate. We are not missing our flight on account

of her lack of common sense and overall
unawareness. We board; I pass out. We land, get to
my car, and are heading home. I drove, so I have to
take everyone home. It is late and I am in need of
some alone time. The drive to drop off Holly and
Gwen at their homes seems to take an eternity.
They lived on opposite sides of the city, and I lived
on another side. I get them home, and finally arrive
home to my Dad's, where I am living at the time.
He meets me at the door and helps with my
luggage.

"Did you have fun?" He asks with a filter-less
cigarette hanging out of his mouth.

"Yeah, I did."

He puts my luggage in the living room and opens a
beer. I light one of his cigarettes and also drink a
beer.

I finish my beer, walk to my room and collapse in my bed. I still smell like a New York City taxicab.

'Do you like it in the ass?'

A Man Created 69ing

Lynette: "Did you 69 this weekend?"

Me: "No. Did you?"

Lynette: "A little."

This conversation became a regular routine for us in the backroom of the salon when we would get bored and delirious from the long day and my occasional neurotic client that Lynette hated to shampoo. Sometimes when the general public is close to sending you over the edge with their unrealistic expectations and inexcusable lateness, all you have left is to laugh about awkward sex positions. We would joke about it because the whole term and concept of 69 is so fucking stupid. News flash: women fucking hate 69ing. It is the stupidest thing ever. We have no pressing desire to be all up in your nut sack, upside fucking down, with your dick in our mouth, with an up close and personal view of your asshole and taint hair, all the while getting eaten out by you, with *our* assholes right in your fucking face. There is too god damn much to concentrate on and we feel just a slight bit of embarrassment and fear of, any given moment, blowing a fart right into your face because our ass cheeks are spread apart. This isn't fun and is always the dude's idea—always. They must think it is hot, or we will enjoy it and really get into it because they saw it on some low budget porn they have had since high school. Not so much. The concept of a two-for-one is bullshit, and we can't wait for the humiliation to be over with.

Me: "Did you get butt fucked?"

Lynette: "Yeah." *Laughter.*

Butt sex is the all-time worst experience that a woman can have. If a woman really likes butt sex, she is a skank or more likely on a serious amount of mid-grade to good ecstasy, a gallon of vodka floating through her blood, blown and numb from the eight ball in her head and no less than a trough of lube on hand and ready to go. All of these criteria are required for butt sex to even be considered by a non-butt-sex-loving woman, so you get the picture: it doesn't appeal to us. Not to say that it hasn't been done under those conditions. The only two women I have ever met who claim to "love" dick in their ass have been around the block a few hundred times, and I'm calling bullshit on that claim anyway. We often joke about butt sex in the back room because it is so gross and perverse, and the sad thing is, almost each and every one of us has a butt sex, or ass play horror story that we have all been compelled to share with each other at some time, usually over a plate of coke at 5 a.m. like back in the old days. Either way, we don't need class-A drugs anymore to discuss and compare butt sex stories. Now the difference between this conversation and someone coming to work and really—like really— telling us their tales of sexy times with their significant other, is that the butt sex conversation is seen as a joke. We can laugh about it, because what is more funny than envisioning your co-worker being butt fucked? It's so ridiculous it's funny. Not funny is telling us that you and your rotund boyfriend made love in a hot tub at the mountain condo you rented for the weekend…and being serious about it. Now, that's just shit you keep to yourself. I don't know what sort of reaction one would want from sharing that information, but the last thing I want to know about is you and your man-piece fucking. Grotesque.

We have to go to bed

The subject of surfaces off of which we have snorted lines came up one day. This is not an unusual conversation to have with the group of people we in the hair industry work with. I think it was Cameron who brought it up. I believe we were talking about Sheila's boobs and big boobs in general, and the story about when Trevor did a line off of Vanessa's tit in Vegas came up. The salon had decided to close down for a weekend and head to an annual hair show. At the time, I was unhappily engaged, but loyal: a virtue not everyone else I work with could claim as true. I was twenty-seven and still had quite the wild hair up my ass, or more accurately, a straw up my nose and a drink in my hand. Vanessa and I were chomping at the bit to get our party on in Vegas, although I had never led on to be as unhappy as I was. Inside, I felt as though I had made a terrible mistake by getting engaged and signing up for the marriage I knew would make me eternally miserable. I had sold myself short and compromised every last thread of my being for Derik. He had voluntarily taken on the role of pseudo-dad to his ex-girlfriend's child: a child that was not biologically his. Noble? Yes, I suppose. However, it always felt as if he still had one foot in that past life of being a "dad." This—I later realized but had always known—was not my problem. It was the problem of his mother who had chosen to make a baby with a stranger at the age of twenty-five. This added stress and the looming and dreaded obligation of having one's child constantly in my home had made me resent Derik. Maybe resentful is an understatement. During our time together, it became apparent that the only thing Derik and I had in common was our love of drinking, and most of his friends did blow, so that was convenient for me as well. Plus, it made coping with a very unhappy engagement and the fact that I had turned into one of those women I hate much more tolerable because I could just become numb to it whenever I wanted.

The trip to Vegas would take me to a place where I could forget about it all. It was a fun city, and Derik never wanted anything to do with it. I felt as if this weekend would get me back to feeling like myself again, eight ball in face and martinis and all. When we landed late Friday night, we urgently needed to find some blow. This was post-911, and carrying a fist full of party favors was now risky behavior.

A few of us had just eaten an amazing meal with several rounds of drinks. True to form, although I bottled it up, I was beginning to jones for a line immediately, if not sooner. I always got this craving after one-and-a-half-drinks. I learned in recovery therapy years earlier that there is, in fact, a chemical response in people that goes off in the brain of a cocaine addict after they consume alcohol. I obviously had not stayed sober after my therapy, and deep inside considered every drink, line and pill a relapse. The mental anguish that was constant, yet hidden, is indescribable. So I numbed myself, and drank more to hide my feelings of failure. The part of recovery therapy about the chemical craving that occurs in the brain had always stuck with me. I thought about it every time I craved that white shit.

After we finished our dinner and met up with the girls, I was on Vanessa's ass to get us some blow. She had connections in Vegas, and I was going to make sure and well that those were utilized. We were hanging out in a bar with a jukebox playing hits from the 80's: Sting, George Michael, that sort of thing. It wasn't the worst setting, but was a little on the dull side for what we were after. After what seemed like an eternity, Vanessa said her friends had texted her, and we met them around the corner. I forget the details, but I think the plan was to go to the hotel and do a *little* coke, then maybe go out again. It was already 2 a.m., but we were in Vegas for work, and we wanted to rage and get fucked up. At least I did. And to be honest, I could have been fine going out all night and all morning and just making a brief appearance at the show the next day.

Vanessa scored the little baggie of my own personal heaven, and I was anxious with excitement. Nothing is like that first line... *nothing.* When you are drunk, or at the very least have a buzz, and your body and soul physically and mentally cannot and, in most cases, oh-so-stubbornly will not go on without that immediate numbing and calming effect, the first moment it hits your nose is filled with ecstasy and relief. Relief that you will no longer be so drunk, and relief that your body and brain just got the fix it needed. The whole process makes me anxious just thinking about it. This process was only a cab ride away. A gaggle of us wound-up, drunk girls rolled up to our hotel and were probably very loud and even more obnoxious. I was originally supposed to be rooming with the owner of our salon and my boss, but that just didn't quite fit into my plan snorting lines and drinking from the mini-bar. So, instead

Vanessa, Trevor, Melissa and I went to Melissa and Trevor's room. We turned on the radio on the alarm clock and busted out the blow. Trevor, new to the whole drug scene, was eager and curious and had only done coke a few times. We were professionals. Melissa chopped out some lines, and I think I had the idea that Trevor—or all of us— should do lines off of a bible we would place on Vanessa's tits. If her boyfriend had any idea that it was now almost 4 a.m., or after (who knew?) and we were snorting coke off of a bible that was balancing off of his girlfriend's tits, he would probably ring her neck. We did line after line and did our best to reserve some blow for the rest of the weekend. If you've ever done coke before, and learned to like it and ultimately depend on it for the sake of having a decent time for the rest of your night, you know that there is nothing worse than running out...especially when you reach that point when you know you are coming down, yet you are secretly crawling out of your own skin. Not even the inhalation of every last cigarette on the planet will soften the blow of coming down from coke or the massive depressions that follow. It's like a collision of all of your worst thoughts crashing into a fire pit. It burns, hurts, and is so loud internally; it's deafening. So, knowing that this feeling was approaching, I kept drinking. We all did. It's the only way to keep going. The mini-bar was running dry, and although I hid it, I was panicking inside. The collision was imminent.

We were also smoking like it was our job and thought we were being considerate by opening the one tiny window in the room. Vanessa, the mother hen of the group, drunk and slightly high herself, swiftly reminded us that it was 5:30 a.m., or maybe it was 6:00, and that the show started at 8:00.

"We have to go to bed." she reminded us. Blank looks of terror washed over our faces, and my half-lit cigarette nearly fell out of my mouth.

Two things a coke addict hates to remember, let alone be told, is that the sun is coming up and that the place you have to be, you have to be in two hours. The day would be long. But, at least we were in Vegas—away from our realities at home. One thing I always tried to do was convince others, and ultimately, myself, that I was not as hung/blown over as I really was. (Blow-over is a term we use for being on a coke hangover. You know, that tweaked-out, shaky, nose-running feeling). The rest of that weekend would be a cocaine-filled shit show, ultimately ending with me feeling a lifetime of regret and guilt.

Under the Influence

I used to come to work drunk all the time. Well, still drunk from the night before, that is. In our industry, it's sometimes the standard. Reconvening in the back room of the salon, and dishing out the details of the prior night was almost like a competition. Whoever made the worst decisions in the worst places with the worst people, won, with the consolation prize being the target of gossip for the salon for that day, and if you really made a mess of yourself, then you won for the week. And we all relished it. Deep down, we all liked being the winner of the craziest story, and along with that, the topic of the salon conversations for the day or week.

Working in a downtown salon at a young age had elevated my standards for many things that I had never even thought of before. Prior to working amongst the refined and grown up, I hadn't given much thought to what kind of vodka I should be drinking or what brand of clothes I should be drinking said vodka in. I didn't come from money, so spending money on designer clothes to be seen drinking designer drinks in was something that simply wasn't thought of. I was always fashionable, but it wasn't until I was exposed to trendy labels that I quickly became the person that would sooner die than wear anything less than euro-designer brands while going out on the town making a complete and utter mess of myself. If you're going to get blackout drunk and coked out of your skull, you better be doing it in European designer clothes, as if that made one look like any less of a disaster.

It was around the age of twenty-three that I really started to care about what my body looked like and what kind of clothes I put my body in. This foolish mindset would begin to cost me a small fortune. It was also around this time that I was *the* female on the scene. I knew everyone from everywhere, and god forbid I let these people see me in a repeat designer outfit drinking designer vodka and doing designer drugs. It was also at this time that I developed a bad habit of not eating before going out. If I had plans on a Saturday night, and I was going to be featuring my ultra-low-rise designer jeans and designer crop-top, I'd rather be a tiny bit dizzy throughout the day due to hunger than have a tiny bit of fat exposed on my already petite frame (as if a Nicoise Salad would impact my body in such a way that I'd go from a petite frame to obese within hours of going out). So, I wouldn't eat. If I did, it was a meal of my morning coffee to wake my likely hung-over ass up and perhaps a very small salad early in the day. This habit of consuming sparse amounts of what rabbits eat, coupled with binge drinking designer cocktails, would always result in me spending the following morning trying to piece together the night prior by looking at my credit card receipts and deciphering drunk texts and looking at my call log. Sometimes I woke up with a small baggie of coke in my bra, not having any recollection of how it got there.

Spencer and I had had a somewhat bad falling out due to my bad decision-making while under the influence of, I believe, vodka, a few pills of ecstasy, and the usual baggie of cocaine. This episode—that I single-handedly caused—was so traumatic and painful for him that he moved to the Hawaiian Islands for eight months to get away from it all. It took me over a decade to forgive myself for the unforgivable pain I caused him, and often out of guilt, I always thought of him as the one that got away. He was. He ran the hell away after I tore his heart out and threw it in a blender. This is a telltale indication of how fucked up I actually was at the time of our explosive break-up. It wasn't that I didn't realize how I'd hurt him, or what I did; I was literally too fucked up on drugs and alcohol to piece it all together and let it marinate. I would be so lost in the depths of trying to fuel my addictions to vodka and cocaine that he became a lost thought. Drugs and alcohol took priority. I would have run away from me, too.

After his hiatus from life here at home, Spencer
had planned a homecoming. It was a Friday night,
and my friends and I, who happen to be mutual
friends of Spencer, had plans to go out to a few
bars. I was giddy with anxiety to see him, not only
to see his reaction when he saw me, but to get back
into his good graces. I was always so madly
attracted to him. Why on earth I fucked him over
so badly, and how the whole situation went down
always replayed in my head like a bad movie with a
bad ending. And each time I wished the ending
would change. I was nervous and excited and, in a
perfect world, he'd forgive me of all my
wrongdoing and welcome me back to his life with
open arms. This was a huge night. Such a
monumental occasion called for a new pair of
designer jeans, a new blouse, and a pair of heels.
The occasion also called for the near-starvation
trick to take full effect in order to have the flattest
of all flat stomachs to show off to my ex-boyfriend

of whom I'd done so wrong (because that will most certainly send him flying back to my arms).

The designer outfit had been purchased for close to $500 from the boutique down the street from where I worked. Money was no issue at the time because I was living with my dad rent-free, and saving money was something I had never been taught. At twenty-three, I was making a very good living. However, most of it went up my nose and into my closet. These seemed like logical locations for my money at the time because of where my priorities were, and quite honestly, I'd never lived a life where I could buy whatever I wanted whenever I wanted. So, to spend $500 on an outfit made me feel like I had "made it," that I was doing what I was supposed to be doing at my age. And, if this gave me a return on my investment in the form of a rekindled relationship with an ex-boyfriend I'd hurt so badly, well then it was certainly worth it.

The night came, and although I was feeling a little lightheaded from only eating a few grapes that day, I disguised that feeling by lighting up a cigarette while driving over to the bar at which Spencer was scheduled to make his homecoming. I was hoping he'd come soon, because true to form, I'd also planned to meet some fellow scenesters at a new and fabulous martini bar downtown that I just *had* to be seen at...in my designer outfit, of course.

I pulled up to the bar. My friends were already inside, and I strutted right in. For some reason, Spencer chose a sports bar in the suburbs for his homecoming. A friend owned it, and it sounded like he wanted something low key. I walked in and stood out like a sore thumb. Everyone was in cargo shorts and baseball caps, and I was wearing sunglasses indoors with rose-colored frames. Wearing sunglasses inside was the thing then. I decided to take them off because I'd done a meticulous job on my eye shadow that night, and I couldn't let that go to waste. But I was looking the best I'd ever looked, or at least I thought so. Looking back, I probably looked like an anorexic member of an all-Latina dance team, featuring eyebrows that were just a tad too thin and skin that was a tinge grey from my steady diet of cigarettes, vodka, and regrettable decisions. Not to mention, I was quickly buzzed from drinking a vodka soda on an empty stomach. The slurring came on fast that night.

Todd and Sofia were the couple I went out with that night. Todd was Spencer's best friend, and Sofia was Todd's girlfriend. Sofia and I had become close friends, so it was both natural and intentional that I would be there on Spencer's homecoming night. But there was one problem: true to form, Spencer didn't show up. The clock was ticking, and I had arranged to meet some friends a new trendy bar downtown. Or at that time, it was called a 'lounge'. Everything was a 'lounge,' which really meant it was a bar like any bar, yet it was just decorated with cheap white

couches and the lighting was blue. I can't
remember the name, but I do remember it was a
one-syllable name of either a color or a fruit. That
was another trend then, too.

I told Todd and Sofia I had to get going. They
agreed that we were all too overdressed for the
suburban sports bar and that we should be seen at
the new lounge. Again, it was named after a fruit or
color, but to this day the name escapes me.

The first thing I did at the single-syllable bar was
order a martini, then another. I mingled with the
fellow scenesters that I was there to meet. We were
still warming up for the night. From here, we'd go
dancing. Mind you, I had no idea it was close to
eleven o'clock at night. I was roughly three
martinis, three vodka sodas, and a half-pack of
cigarettes deep—on a relatively empty stomach. I
loved to dance, and since I was hiding my
disappointment at not seeing Spencer by drinking
my body weight in vodka, I figured, fuck it: let's go

to the club and go dance the night away. My first client the next morning was at 9 a.m. I was just slightly concerned, but I had youth on my side. If I had my usual Saturday morning hangover, it was nothing a breakfast burrito and Pepsi couldn't take care of.

Half—well—mostly drunk, I drove to the club where we'd spend the rest of our Friday night in our designer clothes drinking expensive vodka and being seen by all the right people. I parked the car in the lot across the street from Sway, the latest and greatest nightclub of the moment. Truth be told, I had a huge crush on the door guy. He liked to brag that his dad owned the club, and I'm sure his good looks led to a lot of pussy being thrown at him. A few short weeks later, I'd fuck him on the rooftop of one of his dad's other nightclubs.

I mildly flirted with the door guy in my designer outfit, and Todd and Sofia followed me in. The club was packed, and, of course, I knew the DJ. He was an estranged friend of my ex, Rico. Rico had, as he was known to do, burned a bridge with him, and they had a falling out. His name was Carlos, although he took after the white side of his heritage. He looked like the whitest white boy from the Midwest, but he was fluent in Spanish and had that Latino male protective quality about him. Even though I was the ex of a former friend of his, I was much younger than he and Rico, so he treated me like his little sister. I was now twenty-three, but I had met Rico and his friends when I was sixteen. Carlos, or DJ Los, always kept a stern eye on me if he saw me out. It was like he'd seen my transformation from abused girlfriend to girl-about-town with an ever-growing and wicked drinking and drug problem. Being a DJ, he'd seen it all, and now looking back, it was very endearing that he kept an eye on me when he could. I'd learn later in life that these people are sent to us from the divine or something. This night was no exception.

The last few moments of the night that I remember were 'Los giving me a hug and me ordering a Kamikaze shot. I was still drowning my sorrows at not seeing Spencer that night, but instead of expressing that through conversation, I hid my feelings and self-medicated with shots. I'd do this for the next seven years to shove emotional trauma and sadness over my past down as far as I could push them. The irony is that those feelings never actually go away. All the martinis in the world won't do what actually facing your shit head-on will do. Everything resurfaces. Using vodka as an emotional numbing agent only lasts until you wake up from a blackout. Then it starts all over again. The remorse, headache, drunken confusion, and embarrassment. And then to make it all go away because it was too much to handle in the revolving door of my own thoughts, I'd drink, rinse, and repeat, all to a steady beat of house music among blurry faces.

I opened my eyes. My head was pounding, but I felt happy and good. I knew this feeling. I loved this feeling. I was still drunk. I loved being drunk. The room was dark and unfamiliar, but the sunlight was creeping through the drapes. I was lying on the bed, much like a corpse, wearing all my clothes. My wedge platforms were still on my feet, and my purse was still slung over my shoulder. My rose-colored glasses were still on my face. Crooked, but on my face. I looked around, and quickly realized I wasn't home at my dad's house. I wasn't at Todd and Sofia's, either. I had no fucking clue where I was. I quickly panicked and fished around for my phone. I had no idea what time it was or where I was at, but the thing I did know for sure was Lucy Davis was my 9 o'clock appointment, and I needed to shower off the stench of last night's escapade before I stepped into the salon.

I gathered my things, got off of the bed that I was lying on, and, still drunk, stumbled out of the bedroom. I looked at my phone, and it was 7:00 am

Thank the sweet Lord I hadn't overslept in this strange and unfamiliar room. I opened the door, and saw 'Los sleeping on the couch. Still drunk and giggly, I asked him where I was.

"You were a fucking mess last night. Did you get roofied? I had to carry you out so you wouldn't get kicked out. You couldn't even stand or talk. Do you even remember leaving? I brought you with me to my place because you couldn't fucking talk clearly enough to tell me where you lived. I drove you in your car because you almost drove." I could tell 'Los was equally annoyed at and fearful of my behavior. The truth was, I couldn't remember a thing past that Kamikaze shot, but I wanted to play it cool. I was completely blacked out, but I never liked to admit to that, because then that would mean that I had a problem. And, at that time, I was very much in denial of the fact that I had a serious drinking and drug-abuse problem.

"Yeah, I remember. Of course! Thank you for taking me. Dude, I have to get going. I have to work in a couple of hours." I headed toward the door with a slight stumble.

"You have to fucking work? How?" 'Los asked. I must have looked a mess.

"Dude, I'll be fine. Everyone will be hungover at work today." I saw myself out to avoid a lecture, and to look at the street signs to figure out where the fuck I was because I was too ashamed to ask 'Los.

I stepped out to my car and looked at the street signs. I was on 37th and Navajo in the Northside, not too far from 1st and Wolff where I lived with my dad in the Westside. I started the car, put in a mix CD from one of my DJ friends, lit a cigarette, and drove home. I felt unstoppable. The sun was out, I had a busy day ahead of me at work, and I looked flawless last night (with the exception of me being carried out of a nightclub, of course). So, in my cheery mood, I decided to call one of my gay friends.

"Dude, what the fuck are you doing?" Ethan answered. He sounded fucked up.

"Dude, I'm driving home from my homeboy's house. Apparently I passed out there. I have to go to work. He said he had to carry me out of Sway, but I don't remember that." My song was on, so I turned up my stereo.

"I'm at a fucking party still, and there's a jumpy castle. I ate a few biscuits last night, and I'm rolling my face off," Ethan whispered. He was experiencing the ecstasy paranoia that takes place when you start to come down. We used the term 'biscuit' in reference to ecstasy. It's a rookie mistake to use the actual name of the drug on the phone. Given the fact that a large part of my circle at that time were drug dealers, you could never be too careful on the phone.

"A jumpy castle!? I'll stop by before work. I'm at home now. Let me shower and I'll be over. Where are you?" I asked as I flicked my cigarette in the street in front of my dad's house. I was pulling in just past 7:00 am on a Saturday morning before I had to be at work by 9:00 o'clock. My dad wasn't home. He was at his girlfriend's house, likely partaking in his own fair share of alcohol and drugs. I'd later learn that he and his girlfriend and her friends would stay up all night day drinking and doing drugs that make you stay up all night and day. This was my reality. So, for me to come home on a Saturday morning after having barely survived a night of blacking out was nothing alarming. It was quite normal, actually.

Ethan told me he was at his friend Daphne's. I'd head over there after I got ready. I was out of cigarettes after all, and I knew he'd have a pack.

I showered, put on my designer jeans from the night before, and started to apply my makeup. Then it hit me. I was completely shit-faced. I was wasted. Standing in my bedroom at my dad's house, applying my designer makeup to my tired and drunk face, I thought this was funny. But I was drunk from the night before, and had clients from 9 a.m. to around 5 p.m. It was almost 8 o'clock, and I was hammered. I needed a cigarette. In my condition, there was no way I could choke down food now to absorb the alcohol.

I got in my car, and very responsibly watched how I drove. I easily could have been picked up for a DUI. I smelled badly of alcohol, and my first client was in about an hour.

Luckily, Daphne's house was about ten minutes away. I pulled up and saw Ethan chain-smoking on the porch in a long, fur coat and dark sunglasses. It was mid-July, already over eighty degrees, and this motherfucker was in a fur coat…on a porch…smoking…ten feet from a jumpy castle where our friends were jumping and smoking and also coming down from their night of ecstasy. I wasn't that stupid. I might still be drunk and on my way to work, but I'd *never* eat pills the night before work. I was smarter than that.

"You look like shit and smell like the bus." Ethan said, handing me a cigarette.

"I'm still drunk."

"You look drunk," he said, lighting a cigarette and chewing on the side of his mouth in the way people coming down from good ecstasy do.

"Fuck. Well, maybe I'll have Drew the Dealer swing by and bring me some coke. I need a line to sober up." I texted Drew the Dealer, and he agreed to meet me at my car at the parking garage where he would deliver the cocaine I deemed necessary to get through my day. I knew within an hour or so, I'd sober up and my relentless hangover would kick in, and I had a lot of hair to do. I even had a bride scheduled for her wedding, and my messy ass was doing her makeup.

With little time to spare, I hopped in my car, drove to the parking garage near the salon, and met Drew the Dealer. We quickly made the exchange, and I hurried my still-drunk self to the salon. Thank the sweet Lord above our manager took the day off. She was no stranger to the wild ways of most of the salon staff, but coming to work shitfaced with glossy eyes and liquor seeping out of every pore was not the level of professionalism we were shooting for at the salon.

"What the fuck happened to you?" Eddy, the moody homosexual of the salon, snarked.

"The same thing that happened to you," I barked back.

"Child, you are a damn mess. Put my glasses on."
Now, if Eddy said I was a mess, I was a fucking
mess. I giggled a bit, but inside I panicked. Real life
was happening in the salon. Clients were coming in
to get their hair done. Clients who had normal
mornings consisting of reading the paper and
drinking their coffee after their morning run. I had
a morning of waking up in an unfamiliar place and
buying cocaine before 9:00 am.

"God. I'm drunk. I'm going to go do a line in the
bathroom." I put his high-end sunglasses on, went
to the bathroom, and did a key bump in the stall. I
was soon fresh as a daisy. I wasn't actually fresh as
a daisy. I was high, and that gave me the
impression that I was fresh as a daisy. In all reality,
I stunk like booze, and was now talking too fast
because I was high on coke at 9:00 am.

My first client arrived, and aside from having my
assistant do most of the work, I somehow managed

to apply color to and cut her sparse head of hair. I also managed to style it better than expected. Seeing how I was starting to sober up and transition into the hangover phase, this was a surprising feat. The coke helped. Or at least I thought. Everything is jaw-dropping when you're high on uppers, even your shitty work after a long night of drinking.

My next client arrived, and thank god this was just a women's haircut on a client I didn't know too well that luckily didn't speak to me. She was nondescript, miserably married, in terrific shape, and just wanted to read gossip magazines when she came in. Perfect. She requested an angled bob, which just happened to be my favorite haircut to do and the cut I did best. She worked for a local radio station but was still seen in the public eye. I couldn't let my hangover fuck up her hair. Not her, of all people. She must have been half-blind or just completely oblivious, considering she didn't take note of my condition—or I was becoming way too good at concealing my dirty habits (probably the latter). I'd come into work after doing coke by myself all night sometimes, and no one had a clue. It was a secret I hid very well.

It was after her cut that I started to suffer through the detox portion of my hangover. I could feel the color leaving my face, and I started getting shaky and hot and cold. I felt like I had to throw up. What I was going to puke up exactly, I didn't know? My last meal had consisted of the little bits of grapes I ate the day before. That didn't stop me. I dashed to the bathroom, stuck my fingers down my throat, and puked up neon-yellow bile. Puking up bile means there is nothing left in your stomach but acids. There might have been remnants of a kamikaze shot in there, but it was mostly neon yellow foam. I felt slightly better. I had to pull my shit together because the bride client I had scheduled for wedding makeup was arriving in fifteen minutes. I opted out of doing another key bump of coke because my body was at the point where any more toxins would make me violently ill. I'd done that to myself countless times, but fifteen minutes before a bridal makeup application was not the time to partake in blow. I took a deep breath, rinsed my mouth out, and started chomping on two pieces of gum.

Trying to conceal my detox shakes and the stench of pricey vodka seeping out of my toxic-dump of a body, I spritzed some perfume on and sauntered up to the front waiting room to greet and grab the bride-to-be. I was shaking, and I could feel the cold sweats start and stop.

Luckily, we had done a practice run of her makeup, which meant I had a piece of paper with a sketch of a face printed on it that I had filled out accordingly. My notes told me what I applied and where I had applied it. I greeted her with the obligatory wedding questions: "Are you excited? Nervous? You're going to look amazing!" The only way this woman couldn't have smelled the trough of vodka I drank the night before and the remnants of vomit on my breath was if she didn't have a nose on her face, which wasn't the case. I'm sure I smelled like a dumpster after a frat party…or probably worse.

I was detox-shaking like a leaf on a tree in the wind. I could feel my body swing between cold and hot while I was applying the last of her waterproof mascara. This poor woman. She was paying top dollar on her very special day to have some fucked-up hairdresser/makeup artist do her makeup. Somehow, by the grace of god, I was able to achieve successful results. It wasn't my best work, but it was the best I could do given my self-induced condition.

Even though it was all fun and games from the outside, I knew I had a serious problem. Doing coke at work to sober up? It wasn't like I was the first to ever do this—and certainly not the last—but I was completely out of control, and I knew it.

I wasn't my chipper, tipsy self by the end of the day. The alcohol depressions had started kicking in, and not only was I full-on-hungover, but I was also coming down from the coke I'd done earlier in the day.

I had one last client: a men's cut on a fellow party friend of mine in the scene. He was a high-profile attorney with a penthouse loft down the street and an affinity for strippers and drugs. We were instant friends when we met. His name was Roger. Since I had crossed the client/stylist boundary with him by doing key bumps of ecstasy in his sex swing at an after party, I figured being hungover and coming down from coke was no big deal.

"Girl, you are shaking like crazy. Are you sure you can cut my hair?" Roger asked. I felt horrible inside when he asked me that, like I was such a failure. But I had to laugh it off.

"I'm fine. You're my last one. I'm not that hungover," I said, totally downplaying my state. "I just need to eat and I'll be fine," I replied.

"What did you get into last night? I was at Frame. We had a booth and a bottle, but I was mellow. I only did a few lines and went home," Roger said of his much more tame evening. *Only a few lines.*

"The last thing I remember was doing a shot at Sway. I woke up at a friend's house, and that's that. I'm ordering a pizza when I get home."

"Are you going out tonight? We have a table at Orchid Walls. Have you been? It's just like the clubs in Miami." That was such a thing to say back then. "It's just like the clubs in <insert city>". That was also a trend at the time. Describing a new lounge or club like it was a lounge or club in a different city. Just as long as it wasn't like a lounge or club in Denver.

"Yeah, I was at the opening. It's cool, but the music sucks. They're doing everything on computers now. You know I prefer vinyl," I said as I scattered some pomade through his bleach-tipped hair.

"Well, if you get a wild hair, I'll put you on the list," Roger said, leaving me a generous tip and walking out the salon door.

My day was over…finally. My nose was running from the coke, I felt like absolute shit, and all I wanted to do was wash my face, smoke a cigarette, and order a pizza. I couldn't smell because of the coke, but I probably smelled of old vodka and hair spray.

"Girl, go take a shower and wash off your bad decisions," Eddy quipped as I went to the desk to check out for the day.

I collected my tips and headed home to my dad's. I didn't know if he'd be awake or not. During this time, he and his girlfriend were partying pretty hard, and he often recovered during the day by sleeping it away. That would be ideal because then I wouldn't have to face him in my embarrassment, and it would save me the feeling of knowing that my dad and I simultaneously were battling substance problems. But, like all things with my dad, it was best just to act like our problems didn't exist.

I walked in the door, and my dad wasn't in the kitchen smoking a cigarette in front of the T.V., so he must have been sleeping. I didn't want to have to see him in my state anyway, so this was fine.

Moments after I ordered a pepperoni and extra-jalapeño pizza and a two-liter bottle of soda, my cell phone rang. It was a number I didn't recognize.

"Hello?" I answered as I took a long drag off one of my dad's cigarettes.

"Is this Andrea?" I knew immediately who it was. It was the door guy from Sway.

"It is." Fuck. How the hell did he get my number?

"Hey, it's Giovanni, from Sway. Do you remember giving me your number last night?" My heart sunk. I had absolutely zero recollection of that event.

"Yeah, I totally remember giving you my number! How are you?" I lied, taking an even longer drag off my shitty cigarette.

"You do? You were pretty twisted last night."

"Yeah, I was. Too many shots." Again, I laughed it off.

"Well, what are you doing tonight? I've got you and your girls on the list at Glow if you guys want to go. The night is on me." No wonder he had pussy thrown at him all the time. He was Italian, good looking, and had a key to the city.

I pondered his offer. Do I eat my pizza and rest my ass? Or do I do a costume change and have a fun night out with the Italian door guy I had a crush on? Spencer, my long lost romance, was nowhere to be found, after all, and it was Saturday night.

"I'll see you tonight at Glow. My girls and I will be there." With that, I hung up the phone, took a disco nap, and got ready for the night. The best part was, I didn't have to work the next day—not that it would have mattered. My life was a cycle of drink, snort, smoke, puke, repeat. That night would prove no different.

People still get married?

The Bride

Over the years, I have done hair and makeup for many weddings. Many hairdressers are anti-wedding and for good reason. Not all, but some brides can be such bitches and pains-in-the-ass that you get jaded and do not want to discuss another updo or veil ever again.

One Saturday when I was working at Chic, I had a new non-request updo appointment on my books. I figured that it was for prom or something because no bride in her right mind would schedule an updo without doing a practice run first. Well, I stood corrected in my assumption.

An Asian woman comes in, veil in hand. I have her sit down in my chair.

"So what are we doing today? Is this a practice run?" I ask.

"No. This is for my wedding today," she says, some underlying bride bitchiness in her voice.

"Okay. Did you have a practice run with another stylist?" I ask, assuming she would have done that.

"No. I have not. I just called and asked them to put me with someone who knows what they are doing," she snaps. *Someone who knows what they are doing?* As if we were a salon of people who specialized in not knowing what we were doing.

"Okay, so what would you like to do?" I patiently ask, knowing that this has the potential to crash and burn before it begins.

"I have a picture." She pulls out a picture that I have seen a million times. It is an updo with a stack of barrel curls piled on top of the head, and a slick, severe side part. She will regret this updo choice in about five years. It is fashionable for the time, but way too over-done and—at that point—just looked ordinary. But, whatever. It's her big day, and she's acting like she's the first woman that has ever gotten married.

"Do you think you can do this?" She asks. Brides have an innate knack of being condescending. Most behave as if they were the first woman to have ever been a bride-to-be, and with this, comes the expectation that everyone should bow down to them, accept their irrational behavior, and then tell them how beautiful they look. As if exchanging vows is a noble cause of some sort.

"No problem. Let's get started." I start, casually. I'm surprised I didn't respond with a sarcastic remark. I slid some magazines that were resting on my station closer to her, in hopes that she'd read the latest gossip and stop talking.

"You don't understand. Nothing has gone right with my wedding," Out of nowhere, she started to vent, "My flowers didn't bloom this morning, and the seamstress stained my dress and tried to cover it up with chalk and now it looks like shit. My fiancé lost the ring, and all of my relatives flying in from Thailand can't make it because their flights got canceled. I need this to be perfect," she vents, applying a thick layer of pressure as she does so.

Fuck, I think. This shit has to be flawless. If it were my wedding and I had bad omen after bad omen, I would probably think that the Universe was trying to tell me something. Like, maybe the Universe is trying to tell this lady that perhaps if she were a nicer person, her precious little wedding and all of its precious little details would come together. Or, perhaps being a bitchy bride isn't attractive and all of those around you are actually floored you found someone to marry your bitchy ass.

I get to work, first sectioning her long, thick, straight hair, then pulling part of it up into a ponytail and setting that ponytail in hot rollers. The remainder of the hair would be sleeked, parted and incorporated later. As the rollers cool, I take them out and start pinning her hair, which now has a curl in it from the hot rollers. As I begin to pin, she looks annoyed. But she has looked this way since she walked in the door.

'Um, can you move that pin? It kind of hurts," she whined, making a face as if she were in excruciating pain, while trying to dig the pin out of her hair. I look at the clock and begin to count down until I take those first sips of a dirty martini immediately after work. People like this is why hairdressers are heavy drinkers.

"Sure, I can move it, but I can't guarantee that that piece of hair will stay like it is supposed to," I tell her. She looks at me as if no one in her life has actually ever *not* let her have her way.

I continue with the updo. I am nervous because this bride-to-be is already on the verge of a meltdown, and if her hair isn't perfect, she will undoubtedly combust in my chair, or take all of her wedding issues out on me.

I am putting the finishing touches on the updo when she pulls out a little bag of sparkly, and might I add tacky, little dragonfly clips. Then she pulls out a little bag of tiny butterfly clips. *All this and your veil?* I think. Wow. Looks as though I will be talking someone off of the over-accessorizing-on-your-wedding-day ledge. I finish the updo and spray the shit out of it. It looks flawless: *fucking* flawless. It's not my taste, but it is flawless. I spin the chair around for her to look at it in the mirror.

"Oh my god," she says. I am expecting her to hate it, but I did my best.

"It's perfect." She managed to crack a smile.

"This is the only thing that has gone right, and it is perfect. Thank you so much. I love it! Do you think I should put the clips in it?"

"Honestly, I think it will be too much with the veil and how involved the actual updo is. I would leave them out and just go with the veil," I say.

"Okay. Whatever you think," she agrees. Her tone has changed. Her doubt in my abilities is now a distant thought, and whatever advice I had to give her, she'd now listen with open ears and a quiet, smiling mouth.

I anchor the veil into her massive updo made of hollow barrel curls. She looks like the princess that she wanted to look like.

"Oh my god! I just love it. Thank you so much. This is the only thing that has gone right," she repeats as she hugs me. There was a bit of a tear in her eye.

Did she just hug me?

She was a challenge, not because of her hair, but because of the circumstance.

I couldn't wait for my post-work dirty martini.

The Russian

Brides and their mothers—actually mostly their
mothers, actually always the mothers—can be
absolute monsters. Usually the brides are so beside
themselves they have just decided to let things fall
into place, as they should. It has actually been a
while since I have had a bitchy bride. I've had a few
bitchy bridesmaids, though. One time I did a
wedding with Eddy that was a party of thirteen
people. The bride was all of twenty-two. She was
the typically naïve young bride who had been
mentally planning her wedding since she was four
years old. It was her day and her time to shine with
her groom-to-be, all on her parents' dime. I can't
think of a better way to flush thousands of dollars
down the toilet than to pay for the wedding of your
twenty-two-year-old daughter to some chubby
Russian guy. The standard and common price of
wedding hair is usually in the one-hundred-dollar
range. Eddy, unbeknownst to me, had quoted the
party of thirteen at fifty bucks a head. This was

made known to me on our way to the house where all thirteen of these girls were hanging out and fussing around. Of course Eddy, being the long-time hairdresser for this family, was working on the bride. I had the privilege of doing the three future sisters-in-law. Two of them had kids, and one of the two with kids was knocked up again. The other one, and I quote from one of the bridesmaid, "will be by the end of the night." So I assume they are a little on the loose side.

Future sister-in-law #1 sits in my chair and wants her hair down and wavy. She was pretty nice and was the one with two kids and a third bun in the oven. She was actually pretty attractive and had dark blond hair and kind blue eyes. If the other two were like her, that would be great. Well, they were not.

Future sister–in-law #2 sits down in all of her tacky, bridesmaid glory. She has an unusually short forehead and long, dark, horse hair. There were endless gobs of her nearly ass-length hair. And what do you know, she wanted it all curled in tiny spirals. This is not wedding hair, but more the hairdo of a young Mexican girl at her right-of-passage celebration known as a Quinceañera.

"I vant it all curled. Curls," short forehead says in her broken English. As she says this, I look at the clock and see that we have about three hours to finish over half of the wedding party. I estimate that curling her hair will take two months…at best.

"Well, you see, you have a lot of hair. What I can do is set some of it on hot rollers and use a curling iron for the rest. I have five other girls to do, so I will do the best I can."

"Okay, but I want curls," she says, as if I didn't understand this the first time.

"Okay. I know you want curls, but what I am saying is that you may not have as many as you want because I have to set some of it on hot rollers. If I do all of it by using a curling iron, it will take too long," I explain. Judging by her blank stare, I can tell that this is not computing, so I just carry on.

I section her massive head of hair from the bottom up. I start curling her three-foot-long hair as fast as the curling iron will let me. It already looks hideous. I can tell by her reaction in the mirror that this is exactly what she wanted. As I am curling and setting, and curling and setting, I ask what she wants to do once this is all curled. I think she will look something like the cowardly lion/Rick James/Little Bo Peep, so hopefully she wants to put some of it back.

"I vant it half back," she says. This is my least favorite style of hair to do. Half-up, half-down with curls all over the place has the ability to make any grown woman look like a junior varsity cheerleader.

"Okay. Do you want any pieces down in the front, do you want it parted off to one side, or do you want it all straight back?" I ask since I am in the home stretch of the massive project of curling and setting and curling and setting.

"I want some of it to go to the side like zis," she says. She grabs her mop of hair and pulls her curls off to one side so they can cascade down in front of her shoulder. As she does this, she begins to remind me of one of those porcelain dolls with the ringlet-curled hair.

"Okay. So do you want it in a ponytail and off to the side, or do you want it pinned?" I ask. This is going to take a while, I can tell.

"I vant it on the side. No bangs. Just all to the side and full in here." She points to her crown. So she wants the three feet of Little Bo Peep/Rick James curls, which by the way have shrunk to a foot and a half, cascaded off to the side, with a side part, and a full crown. This is going to look ridiculous, and yes, it will be Quinceañera hair.

I have begun pinning and placing her curls. The whole time she is sighing…and shifting about…and sighing again…and looking at her sisters…and sighing yet again. I don't have the patience for a grown woman to throw a hissy fit in my chair, so I ask her what the fuck her problem is.

"What's the deal? Do you need me to change something? Tell me now, because once it is sprayed and pinned there is no turning back," I tell her. I have now had her in this chair for an hour and a half. The bride usually takes about that amount of time, if that tells you something, and this mail-order bride is nowhere close to content.

"I vant it more like this." She moves her cascade to her back and lets it fall over her back.

"Okay. So you don't want it off to the side like we discussed? Now you want it back?" I ask.

"Yes. Ugh. I just vant it bigger. And curled."
"Well, it is curled and it is pretty big," I say, pointing out the obvious to her. Needing to be told the obvious is usually a trait I deplore in people, but for the rude bridesmaid/soon-to-be-sister-in-law, it was the only way to get through.

I knew what the problem was. When her hair was all curled and back, it accentuated her half-inch-tall forehead. She looked like she was wearing one of those old-fashioned motorcycle helmets, with all that dark hair and that teeny, tiny forehead. I would be pissed too, if I looked like one of those weird porcelain dolls with the big bug eyes.

"How is this?" I pin her hair in the half up, half down manner she implied.

Another sigh.

"I just vant it bigger and maybe to the side. I don't know," she says.

"So like this?" I give her crown some more volume, which has made her tiny forehead look like a piece of masking tape holding her hair to her head.

"No. Not like this. I don't like it." She whines and fidgets and has now had her hands in her hair for about five minutes. I am losing patience, and need to move to the other girls. Friends of the bride keep checking in and giving me the I'm-so-sorry-you-have-to-deal-with-this-cunt look.

"Well, even if you don't like it, the good news is that it isn't your wedding so nobody will be looking at you anyway," I say, once again pointing out the obvious to her. She shot me a blank stare. As if this whole time she'd thought she was going to be the belle of the ball, and much to her dismay, I'd pointed out that she wouldn't be.

We wrap up quickly and I continue with the other bridesmaids.

I shot Eddy a glare from across the room that read: "You're buying drinks and sushi after this, you asshole." It donned on me that we should have stopped for a drink prior to this.

Controlling Mother-of-the-Bride

Molly had been a client for about a year and a half. She was one of those people that sits in your chair and just clicks with you. She was super nice and appreciative. She has an angelic face with creamy alabaster skin and curly light brown hair and blue eyes. She doesn't require a lot of makeup. Her skin is flawless and she has a kind smile. She is likable and sweet. We always have good conversation, and she is always on time.

Like many of my late twenties/early thirties gals, they get engaged and so begins the hustle and hype surrounding all things wedding. Molly was proposed to with a platinum and diamond ring that was cushion-cut and had a very antique and vintage appearance. It suited her perfectly. She always has had a vintage feel to her look.

We began discussing details of her wedding. She had asked me to go up to Aspen to do her and her mother's hair along with whatever small wedding party she may have. I told her I would be more than happy to go up there; I would just have to take the day off far in advance, being it was a Saturday, industry's busiest day. Asking for a Saturday off from Mark was like asking for his left nut. But, begrudgingly, he gave it to me. I had planned to make a weekend out of it with Derik, so I was actually looking forward to it.

Like with all brides, I suggested doing a practice run. Molly and I had decided to do her practice run about a month prior to her big day. She asked if she could bring her mother, and I said, "of course." I had met her petite mother once before when she came with Molly to a haircut appointment. She seemed normal… "seemed" being the key word. Molly told me that she and her mother were having a disagreement over her dress. Molly was planning on wearing a platinum satin gown that was low in the back with a cowl-neck front. She wanted her hair to be curled with her own natural curl and a low, romantic updo. I thought this sounded right up her alley. She was not going to wear a veil but had some vintage clips for her hair. Her mother wanted her to wear a long-sleeved cream lace dress. This was the disagreement. Molly wanted to wear what she wanted to wear, and her mother wanted her to look like a tacky bride from the late seventies. She probably wanted her to wear a lace hat as well.

The practice-run appointment came and so did her crazy bitch-of-a-mother. Now, understand that Molly had already discussed what she wanted her hair to look like with me. I explained to her that a practice run is not an exact representation of what her actual 'do will look like. It is simply meant to get a feel of what the hair will do, to see how the veil/headpiece/clips and whatnot will look, and to see if any adjustments need to be made to the hair. This gives the bride a pretty good idea of what it will look like without giving away all of my work and secrets before the gig is booked (note: never do shit without getting paid or getting a deposit first). This situation would be my lesson.

Molly and her mother arrive at the salon. Molly looks a little frazzled and annoyed. Uh-oh. This can't be good. I knew in my gut from the get-go that this was going to be a disaster. I wasn't worried Molly would be the disaster; I was worried that her crazy-eyed mother would be. That look is never good. You know the type: the crazy eyes that are there but not quite present, like they are looking through you and things just aren't a hundred percent upstairs. Yea, this was her mother.

Molly sits down in the chair, and we discuss what we have already discussed. Her mother interrupts and is standing right next to us, invading my workspace. I already hate her. I hate anyone who intrudes upon my personal space, especially when that anyone is an interruptive and intrusive cunt like her.

I begin to set her hair like I told her I was going to. This is a normal step in the process.

"Well what are you doing? That doesn't look like you are using her natural curl to me. Why are you using those rollers? Are you going to use any of her natural curl?" crazy bride mom asks, which begins to really irritate me. I can tell Molly is feeling tense but she has yet to tell her mom to settle down.

"This is a practice run, so what I am doing is actually testing out a couple different ways to set the hair so I can decide what will work better," I explain. I am trying to keep my cool, but this woman is breathing down my throat.

"Well, I just don't understand what you are doing. You know, I made these hair ornaments that maybe you can use on the bridesmaids. I'll go grab them. I also brought my dress so you can see what I am wearing so you can get a good idea of what to do for my hair. What do you think I should do to my hair? Leave it down? Put it up? I just don't know. I'll be back. I'll go grab the hair ornaments and some other jewelry I have made. Maybe the girls can wear that too." I'm pretty sure she didn't take one breath during that whole moment.

"I'm so sorry. She is being so difficult and wants to be involved in everything and still is arguing with me about the dress," Molly says. I do feel for her. But, had it been my mother acting like a complete nut job and being an absolute pain in the ass, I would have told her to sit the fuck down or leave.

In comes crazy mom holding a dress on a hanger and a box full of sandwich bags that are full of what appeared to be some sort of arts and crafts project. I am assuming that this is her jewelry and hair-ornament crap—and crap it was. She also had an entire binder of wedding ideas, some of which were actually going to be in the wedding and some just random shit. She sets up camp near my station, invading the space of another stylist. I tell her to keep things in one area and that other people have to work. She looks dumbfounded as if there are actually other people in the world that she may have to be considerate of.

I try to continue to talk to Molly and explain what the set was that I just did. I wrapped her hair on old-fashioned curlers while it was damp to see what it would do. I told her I would probably opt for the other way I wanted to set it, which was to use hot rollers. She seemed fine with this, and we discussed her dress, etc.

"Well, I want to see this other set. Aren't you supposed to do exactly what you are going to do?" Molly's mother rudely asks; at the same time, she has her hands in Molly's hair.

"Why don't you get your hands out of her hair so I can do my job," I bark. She is sending me over the edge with all of her fidgeting about and her hands all in Molly's hair.

"Oh. Well. Okay. I just want to see exactly what it is going to look like. I mean, isn't that the point of this?" she asks as she is pulling some of her "jewelry" out of its sandwich-bag homes. Her "jewelry" consists of string with plastic beads on it, tied together to make a bracelet. Her beads resembled the beads I used to put on my bicycle spokes when I was a kid so they would make a clinking noise. I guess her vision of how Molly should look on her day was this: an ivory, long-sleeved lace dress and a plastic-neon-bead bracelet adorning her head.

"Mom, sit down. We are almost done. Andi, don't worry. I get what you are saying. You don't need to redo my whole hair." Molly finally pipes up with something useful. I think she could tell that I was growing past impatient and her mother was bugging the shit out of me by putting out all of her little bracelets for display on my station, making it look like a kiosk in an airport.

"No, I want to see it the other way," her mom insists.

"Fine. I have a client in ten minutes, but I will do what I can do in ten minutes. I'm telling you, we already discussed what we are going to do; she gets the idea and this is what a practice run is," I tell her as I am setting her hair up a storm with this crazy bitch breathing down my throat.

The air was tense, and the mom knew she had pissed me off. And now, Molly was irritated but still failed to get her mother under control. I continued the best I could to show her a version of the updo that would be used for her wedding. A little fact: I never do *exactly* what I plan to do on the day of. Why? I only give away a taste of my work. I never do a full-on, day-of updo. People steal your work and decide not to book you and be cheap by doing it themselves after they just watched you do it. Of course, it never comes out good. I finished up and escorted them to the front desk. They paid, and I told Molly I would talk to her soon regarding the details of her wedding day.

When I came to work the following Tuesday, there was a message on the voice mail that they had canceled. I knew it. They didn't even have the balls to ask to talk to me. They pussed out, per her mother, and left a voicemail on a Sunday—when we are closed—that they were canceling. This is why I require a 50% non-refundable deposit and signed contract due at consultation to secure the date.

This is also one of the many reasons I was a very heavy drinker at this time. People can be absolute cunts.

Do You See a Therapist?

I looked at my schedule for the day and saw two of my most energy-sucking clients on my books…back to back. This makes for a long day, a day when I'm going to have to dip into my energy and positivity reserves way down deep in the depths of my being to get through these two clients. People really can deplete you of your energy. You can also absorb their energy, whether it's good or bad. It really is fascinating how energetically lifting or draining humans can be.

The first of the two energy-depleting clients was Candace. God love her, Candace has been coming to the salon for five and a half years. During these five and a half years, we have had the same entrance that requires a code to get in. The salon is located in an office building, which is both secure and complicated for a special few. Candace usually shows up to her appointments late, frazzled, and disheveled. Her hair is too long for her age, and very thin. I think she may only have two hairs on her head, but along with her dowdy appearance, it suits her quite well. I look at the clock, and she is already fifteen minutes late. That is my number one pet peeve about working in the service industry. I loathe when people are late. Candace, in addition to being late every time, always brings her kid, which, to anyone that knows me knows that bringing a kid to a haircut given by me is not a good idea. I make no apologies about not being a kid person.

I am sitting at the desk, and the phone rings.

"Salon 182, this is Andi, "I say, suspecting it is Candace.

"Andi?" It's Candace (sounding confused).

"Yes?" I'm already annoyed and running late, and she hasn't even walked in the door yet.

"Andi, the door is locked. I can't get in." We go through this each and every time. And I see this woman every six weeks. You can imagine my frustration.

"You dial 7825." I say, a little annoyed.

"What? I dial what?"

"7825. That's the code that unlocks the door." Fuck, man.

"Oh! Okay."

She scurries in the door less than a minute later, and I scuttle her back to my chair for a very quick consultation. She's stressed out, scattered, and of course doesn't know what she wants. Her son, on the other hand, seems to remember the process, and sits down in a chair in the corner and opens his coloring book. I'm convinced he takes after his dad.

"What would you like to do with your hair today Candace?" I ask, talking and leading her to the shampoo bowl.

"Oh, I don't know. I'm not sure. What do you think? I don't want to lose much length, and I don't want layers. I think the bangs are too long, but what do you think?" She is finally seated at the shampoo bowl. When a client is indecisive about what they want, it's my general rule of thumb to just give them a trim. Now is not the time to do something radically different. Plus, I have less than thirty minutes to shampoo, cut, dry, and fine-tune her cut. I generally take forty-five minutes. Trim it is.

"I think we should shape it up, give it some bounce, and polish the ends up a little bit." All of that is an embellished way of saying: 'I'm trimming a half inch off all over, and drying you as fast as possible because you were almost twenty minutes late.'

"Oh my God! Is that a burn?" Candace asks. She is asking about the red ink tattoo I have on my left inner wrist. She asks this every-other time.

"No, it's a tattoo." I smile, annoyed, and walk away to wait in the back room.

My assistant finishes her shampoo, and I cut both of her hairs in record time. I dry and style them in record time, as well. Just as I'm wrapping up, my next client arrives.

Beth was my second energy-sucking client of the day. It's always hard to predict what kind of mood Beth is going to be in. She can be happy and jovial, or negative and downright bitchy, lashing out at this and that for no apparent reason.

The first time Beth came in, we had a brief consultation. She had super short hair. She has a very small forehead and her short hair made her look like she was wearing a hockey helmet. We had agreed that this was probably not the best look for her and decided to grow it out. Beth expressed that she'd like something different and more up-to-date than her current style and color, a color which resembled the stripes on the back of a bumblebee. She scheduled a color appointment for eight weeks out, and I was excited to give her a medium brown base with caramel highlights.

Eight weeks later, Beth arrives to her color appointment and sits in my chair. This is verbatim:

"My sons both have super curly hair. I have a daughter who has done just about every drug you can imagine. She is adopted. My husband passed away and left me with these three kids. They can be so shitty sometimes. The adopted one is autistic. I had to kick her out when she was younger. She was

192

doing too many drugs and got pregnant. Now, since I am a pro-lifer, we made her keep the baby. Now, she lives with another family with the baby...."

I barely knew this woman, and we jumped right into family secrets and scandal. I took a deep breath and collected myself.

"Okay. So what are we doing with your hair?" I interrupt, swiftly shifting gears to hair. We decided on a medium brown base and caramel highlights that I had envisioned more suitable for her, as opposed to her dated helmet. I tried to evade the pro-life topic as quickly as possible and didn't comment on her daughter's drug usage. I had to keep this appointment flowing.

I colored her hair a medium brown with caramel highlights just as we spoke about. The new color brought a richness and softness to her skin that her previous yellow highlights didn't achieve. She looked pretty. I was satisfied with the work, but it was hard to tell if she was, considering all her chatting about her son who didn't quite meet her expectations and the job that she hated.

I think that's one of the toughest things about this profession. To a certain extent, we are expected to listen and dispense advice and conversation to each and every client and tailor said conversations and advice to their moods and energy. Now, if it's a fun client that makes you laugh, it's fantastic. There's nothing like belly laughing at work, right? But if it's someone that comes in and literally shits negativity out of their mouths and into your chair and drains your energy, well, it pretty much depletes one of all the feel-goods.

Obviously, Beth happens to be one of the latter types of clients. Beth called a few days after her appointment and complained that she wants her highlights lighter. The whole purpose of her coming in was to get a new look and new perspective. Her best friend, perhaps my favorite client of all time, had sent her in. To this day, I'm perplexed as to how those two women have been friends for over twenty-five years.

Beth comes in for her re-do and essentially wants her signature yellow bumblebee stripes back. I point out, that as discussed and requested by her, going back to the yellow, more severe highlights won't achieve the results she had wanted. I got a blank stare. After much discussion, it is clear that she did not, in fact, want a change. I hustle to the back room, mix some bleach, and highlight her hair. All parties are now happy. But I am not happy because of my results with her hair; I am happy that she has now exited the building.

Beth has been divorced for some time and the subject of dating has come up on a few occasions. My strategy is to get her done as soon as humanly possible and nod and smile while ignoring everything she says. Most things she says are inappropriate and awkward, like how she told me she was going through menopause and how her periods are weird and how she can't run when she is on her period because it makes her vagina dry. I could have lived my whole life without knowing that information.

Exactly six-weeks later from the previous encounter, Beth came in for her color and cut appointment, and continued talking about this fellow she had been seeing. I use the term 'seeing' loosely. Apparently there was a city worker or garbage man of some sort that paid her a little attention a while back. The last time she was in she had mentioned that she wanted to slit his tires because he had blown her off after they had sex. Have I mentioned this woman is fifty? And a piano lesson instructor? And looks like a fifty-year old piano lesson instructor? So, I quickly had to advise her not to slash anything of anyone's. At this same appointment she told me she would tell him she was pregnant because they didn't use a condom. "That'll get his attention," she smirked.

The city worker or garbage man or what-have-you comes up at her next appointment, and she is in a tizzy and irritated because she saw him on his garbage truck or city truck or whatever, and he didn't have the nerve to wave at her.

Then she goes into the social-media stuff. By this time, I have about ten minutes left of her color application to go, and these ten minutes are going to slog by. I stir her color and look at the clock.

"I stalked him online and didn't realize that he was into all of this drug stuff. I mean, he was smoking pot in some of his pictures, and I thought, wait till his ex-wife sees those. There goes his custody of his kids. This explains everything. You know, when we had our date, and well...you know...had sex, it was so different than anything I had ever experienced. When I went to his house, he asked me if I wanted some pot, and I said 'no, I don't do pot,' and he said, 'well you have to do something.' I told him I drink wine, so he brought out a bottle of wine that was half empty. I'm not sure what was in it, but within a few sips I was feeling really outgoing and was talking a lot and having a good time. I made him put some music on, and I started dancing around his living room and taking my clothes off. I think I got roofied because I would never do anything like that. Then, we were having sex and he flipped me around and flipped me over. I was with my ex-husband my whole life and we only had sex when my kids were conceived, so I don't even remember how it's done. I didn't know there were other ways to have sex until he flipped me over. It was all kind of blurry, but really fun. I passed out at his place, and the next day I had to teach piano lessons with a horrible hangover. I must be a lightweight. I haven't heard from him since, and I want to go to his house and give him a piece of my mind. I might even leave a nasty note threatening to burn his house down or something.

I might complain to the city and get him fired."
She finally took a breath.

"That is a lot of information," I said. Uneasy and
exasperated from the topic, I sped up my color
application process.

Un-phased, she continues, "I'm really surprised my
vagina wasn't dry. Or maybe it was. I was on my
period, and with my menopause, my vagina gets
dry. But I don't remember because I really do think
he slipped me something in my drink. But maybe I
was drunk. I don't drink that much, so maybe I did
tie one on."

I can handle a lot and do realize that people tell
their hairdressers nearly everything. But, in this
instance, listening to someone my mother's age talk
about their sexual encounters and natural vaginal
lubricant deficiency was crossing a boundary...a
very uncomfortable boundary. Plus, the implication

that something nonconsensual had happened left me in an awkward spot.

"That's a lot of personal information. It sounds like maybe you should talk to someone about it?"

"Well, I'm talking to you about it." She laughed.

"Yeah, well, you know what I mean."

"That didn't make you uncomfortable, did it?" She was half-laughing.

"A little," I say, moving her to a different chair to make room for my other client.

"Do you see a therapist?" I asked her.

"Oh, yeah, I see a therapist," she says.

"Just wondering," I say, reminded of that conversations like these are one of the reasons I drank so heavily for so many years the minute I stepped out the salon door.

Pot Pies (Concluded)

"Andrea," the CA woman started, "I'm very sorry to tell you this."

"Tell me what?" I asked.

"Your dad collapsed today at work." Okay, I am thinking, *tell me which hospital he is in and we can hurry and go get there. He clearly had a heart attack and we need to get to the hospital right away.*

"They tried to revive him. They did mouth-to-mouth and couldn't revive him." I thought *what do you mean they couldn't revive him? Of course they could. You guys just came here to tell me he is in the hospital and just suffered a heart attack.*

"He collapsed today, and he died," the CA said. She had said it. The words I never want anyone close to me to hear anytime soon. He died. My dad was dead. Just like that. He was dead. Everything went silent and slow, but with an indescribable speed. It's not something you completely understand unless you hear those words. Time both stands still and zooms by right at that moment. It sunk in. I always had a feeling my dad would go young.

"NOOOOOOOOO!!!!!!!!!" I cried a breathless scream. I collapsed into Derik's chest. I felt hot and sweaty and cold and shaky and weak. My heart sank into the ground, into the earth, all the way to the other side. I got lipstick all over his t-shirt. The hair on my head felt electric, and my blood went completely cold. I started moving my feet back and forth and rocking back and forth into Derik. The back of my neck tightened up. I couldn't stop pacing and shaking and crying. Actually, I did stop crying. I was in so much shock that my body quit making tears. Nothing was coming out. I could feel my face turn purple. I was going into a state of shock, and simultaneously having a panic attack, although I didn't know it at the time. I would later be able to identify panic attacks with much more clarity. My conversation with my dad from the night before was replaying in my head. *"Don't forget the capers!"*

"I'm sorry to tell you this, but you are next of kin and you had to be told first."

Everything else she said at that point was a blur. I looked into the salon doors, and Melissa was just looking at me like she didn't know what to do. I told her to call Spencer.

I wanted to talk to Vanessa. Derik was there, but I wanted Vanessa for some reason. Derik said we had to go.

We left the salon and Derik and I drove to my dad's. I was in utter shock and could not stop crying. The tears came back, and they didn't stop. Derik asked if I wanted a cigarette. I sure did.

My phone rang, and it was Spencer. I didn't have to answer with the habitual "hello." I just picked up and he asked, "What happened? The salon said it was your dad and you had an emergency and had to go. You never go."

"My dad died today." I barely got the words out. I was trembling, crying, tears rolling down my face, shaking, trying to light a cigarette and trying to talk to Derik all at the same time. Although at that exact time, in that exact snippet of conversation, I knew I was talking to someone who could almost read me over the phone.

"Fuck. What!? Fuck. I'm so sorry." I could hear his pitch change to that pre-cry choke. I heard the tears welling in his throat. With the distance Derik and I felt between us at this time, I wanted nothing more than to be in the presence of Spencer, not in a sexual or attraction sort of way, but in a being-around-someone-who-really-knows-me sort of way. My other line was ringing, and I told Spencer

I had to go. I told him I would call him later, and I really meant that. I wasn't just saying that.

Driving to my dad's house was surreal. I hadn't been there in quite some time. A distance had grown between us. I couldn't tell you now if it was because of his closeted drug use or mine, because of Bernadette, because of my now regrettable disappointment in him, or because of my disappointment in myself. Everything was going in slow motion. I can still see the green grass on the lawns so vividly and feel the snot dripping down my chin, but I was too distraught to care. I didn't even know my own name at this point, let alone take notice of my snot-drenched chin and neck.

We arrived at his house, and I unlocked the door. The house was a mess. There were beer cans and cigarette butts spilling out of numerous ashtrays. This was unsettling not only because it showed in grave detail the state of his addiction, but it mirrored what my own home looked like after a bender. It was too similar. And then it hit me. I'd never hear his voice again. I'd never see him walk through the door again. We'd never share a cigarette again, and talk about whatever we could bring to the surface. That's what makes death so finite. The "I'll never see/hear/do" with that person again. It's over. Just like that, with one phone call or conversation, it's over.

Reflecting on that day, I see that my dad and I were both struggling and hiding a drug addiction and lifestyle that we were too ashamed to talk about and admit to, so we went along pretending everything was fine. I was longing for my dad to come back after the breakup with Bernadette, and I think he was on his way, actually, but the disease of addiction had unfortunately taken the best of him. His lifestyle would ultimately be his demise. But it's more complex than that. My dad struggled with depression. He'd suffered an immense amount of loss in a short amount of time and had never dealt with it. He, like I had done and would continue to do, self-medicated with substances until he was numb and eventually dead.

Though devastated and almost destroyed by his death, I know that he wasn't happy here on earth. He had been the outcast of his family. He never quite fit in. He wanted to so bad, but he had a thing for Chicana women and had two kids at a very young age. He held on to his Westside pride like a medal of honor. He left the hood, but the hood never escaped him. A true Westsider, he was proud. He was more Chicano than our Chicana mother, although he was half German, half Italian. He always related and identified more with his Westside Chicano brethren.

He did his best. I just wish he would have seen in himself what so many people saw in him, but when your head is cloudy, and your spirit is infected with substance, that's impossible. I know because my spirit was clouded and polluted with drugs and alcohol for nearly half of my life. Had I not finally managed to get sober at 30, I could have very well ended up like my dad: a hidden human in hiding; vacillating between sensitive and hard, too numbed and addicted to self-medicating over endless, deep-rooted problems to give living a chance. But it's never too late to fix what is shattered. Once something is shattered, you're free to put the pieces back how you see fit. I did.

To this day I won't eat pot pies.

1,450 Hours

I started beauty school in June of 1995. I was in the
height of my teenage rebellion, and thought I knew
it all. I was determined to be a successful
hairdresser, and nothing was going to get in my
way. In Colorado, you have to complete 1,450
hours to be eligible to take your State Board test to
receive your license. This generally takes about two
years. I didn't want to wait two years, so I made a
few alterations in my current situation. I had been
attending Vogue Academy of Hair Design for the
summer and was only going part time, but I wanted
to go to beauty school full time. I knew that there
was a program at an alternative high school where
students who had a job and took vocational or
college courses could register for their night school
program. That was the ticket. I could complete my
hours in half the time if I went to Vogue Academy
of Hair Design full time during the day and worked
toward my high school diploma at night.

I was currently enrolled at Falcon High School. I loathed, I mean seriously loathed, everything about it, from the cliques to the teachers to the cheerleaders to the subpar cafeteria food I had to eat. I hated it. I didn't actually go that much. I just wanted to do whatever the fuck I had to in order to get out of there. I don't have many good memories of Falcon. I was pretty much a disaster throughout my time there. Looking back now as an adult, I realize I wasn't supervised like a teenage girl should be, and this resulted in me being left to my own devices. Deep down, I knew I had to find some sort of stability for myself. Doing hair would be my ticket to stability. My mother is a hairdresser, and my whole life, I was encouraged to be one too. I was never encouraged to do anything else. College was never encouraged or even talked about by my parents. Actually, I take that back; my dad once suggested I become a female engineer like some of the ones he worked with. That was my only conversation I had with either of my parents about higher education. I never felt like I was smart enough to go to college and get a degree...so I didn't.

I had figured that I wasn't suited for traditional high school, so I decided to withdraw from Falcon and enroll at The Right Path Alternative High School. I would attend beauty school at Vogue Academy of Hair from 8:00 in the morning until 4:00 in the afternoon. From there, I would go to night school at The Right Path Alternative High School from 5:00 in the evening until 9:30 at night. My dad wasn't pleased at all with my new schedule, seeing as how he would have to act as my chauffeur most of the time until I got my license and a car. My friend Debbie would be attending the same night school program, as well as working part-time at beauty school as a receptionist, so we could car pool sometimes.

Don't let anyone fool you: beauty school is the absolute worst part of the industry. I attended a vocational school throughout high school. This means that a lot of the tuition is paid for if you stay in good standing with attendance, grades and such at both schools. Seeing how my dad was always on my ass, I had no choice. I was by no means a perfect student, but I did graduate from cosmetology school early. High school? I graduated a semester late due to my excessive absences at my former high school. I don't think my mom actually cared if I went to school or not, and my dad was too busy with work, struggling to pay his new obligatory child support and alimony.

Beauty school, for me, was a time of learning and exploring. I met a lot of new people. My friend Mary, who I met at Falcon, was also doing the program.

The purpose of beauty school isn't necessarily to hone your craft—you actually learn very little of what you'll actually need as a hairdresser in school—instead you go in order to complete the number of hours required to take your State Board

Test and become a licensed cosmetologist. Once you pass both your written and practical tests, you get your license, allowing you to legally work in a salon.

At the time of my beauty school graduation, I was in a relationship with Rico. We'd been together for about seven months. I'd been hiding it from all of my friends and family for as long as I could, but Rico had gone back to jail for violating probation for his felony drug charges. I was seventeen, and he was twenty-five.

Through his manipulation and verbal abuse, I soon became his source of money and transportation, and the house I lived in with my dad would soon become his place of residence. Because of my past, involving sexual trauma and all of the textbook behavior that comes with it, Rico always held this over my head: no one would ever want me except for him, and if I didn't do what he told me to do— give him rides, let him use my car, give him money, etc.—he'd leave me and tell everyone about my past. This scared me enough to cave into his abusive manipulation. That, and the all-too-often slamming of my head into a wall or the window of my own car. He not only manipulated me into staying with him and being his source of money and shelter, but he scared me into it. He abused me into it. I was a prisoner in my own head and body, as well as in my relationship. While others my age were worried about what they would wear to prom, I was worried my boyfriend was going to hit me if/when I came home too late from school because his jealousy would cause him to assume I was cheating on him. You know what they say: jealousy is a sign of two things—insecurity and/or a guilty conscience. Rico would prove to have the latter.

The time finally arrived for me to take the State Board Test. I was excited and nervous but also relieved that I'd made it this far and Rico hadn't sabotaged me in some way. That wouldn't be far-fetched—for him to somehow mentally and physically abuse me into foregoing my cosmetology license. Every accomplishment I'd achieve was a threat to him. He'd let me know this by slamming my head into a wall, (that was his favorite form of physical abuse), or stealing my car. I was literally living in hell while succeeding beyond my own expectations. I wasn't going to let Rico's abuse impact my ambition. I knew that this was one step closer to finally getting him out of my life. Atrocious humans like him don't just go away overnight. This would take years. I often fantasized about stabbing him to death in his sleep.

The practical part of the exam was held in a vacant space at a local, nearly abandoned mall. The exam would take eight hours, and we'd be tested on our technical abilities to perform different hair services ranging from haircutting, wrapping perms, applying relaxers, and dyeing colors. We were required to bring a model, our ID, and our kit filled with the necessary equipment to perform all required technical services. Should we run out of time on one part of the exam (each service was timed), we'd be disqualified. Not having the required supplies in our kit would also lead to disqualification, as would not having a legal ID. Should any of these things happen, you'd be asked to leave, and you'd have to reschedule your exam and pay the fee the State Board charged to take the exam.

The night before my practical exam, Rico and I had a fight. This was not unusual. In fact, I thought fighting was so normal and regular in a relationship that I didn't think relationships were valid unless there was constant turmoil. I would carry this cycle of manipulation and relationship-behaviors well into my thirties.

Our fight probably stemmed from me not doing something he wanted me to do, resulting in him belittling me and once again reminding me that I was as useless as yesterday's garbage. He was in jail at the time, and because I was about to take my exam and was excited and happy, he felt like I wasn't paying enough attention to his need for constant reassurance and coddling when he was locked up. Our fight and his name-calling and belittling left me crying all night He left me feeling like I was worth nothing. He always made me feel like I was nothing...or at least that I'd be nothing without him.

The morning of my exam, my grandma Lorraine came over. She and I have always been very close, and even though she's tough as nails, she'd do anything for me. She was going to be my model for my State Board exam. She could tell I was distracted, as I was very distant that morning. To this day she knows me better than anyone.

We drove to the exam site and parked. Being the top of my class in school, I was overly confident in my ability to pass the practical exam with flying colors on the first shot. Even though I was distracted by the abusive words of Rico replaying in my head, I was going to take this exam and pass with flying colors. There was no doubt in my mind.

As my grandma and I entered the room where the exam was taking place, I saw a sign that read, "Please have ID ready." I shuffled through my purse, grabbed my wallet, and went to grab my ID. Strange, it wasn't in its normal spot. Even at eighteen, I was a creature of habit with an ever-worsening case of OCD. My ID was always in the exact same spot. I searched my wallet and my purse. I looked in my kit and turned my pockets inside out. I couldn't find it anywhere. I was flustered, frustrated, and embarrassed. From a very young age, I had always put an immense amount of pressure on myself to be perfect—probably because, deep down, I knew I wasn't and wanted to deflect any attention away from my fucked up past.

"Andrea, can you find it?" my grandma asked.

Tears started welling up. "No."

"Oh, Andrea." I felt so bad. My grandma had taken the day to be my model for my exam: an exam that takes eight hours.

"I can't find my ID," I told the woman who was checking for IDs.

"I'm sorry ma'am. You're going to have to reschedule your exam." I was crushed. I had practiced and practiced and was as ready as I'd ever be to take my exam. The next exam wasn't for a couple of weeks.

Watching me cry with frustration and sadness, my grandma said, "Don't worry about it! We'll just come back in two weeks! Stop crying."

I was so disappointed in myself because I knew the fight with Rico the night before had distracted me enough that I didn't double-check that I had everything. It donned on me that I had taken my

ID out to go get cigarettes the day before and had set it on my dresser right as Rico called from jail. I cried all the way home and feared breaking the news to my dad. He was eager for me to take my test and pass so I could start working. I was petrified.

The situation resulting from not being able to take my exam quickly blew over. My dad was a little disappointed in me, but he quickly forgot about it once the weekend came along and he could go to the nightclubs he frequented on Friday and Saturday nights. I had rescheduled my exam, and for the next two weeks, I would compulsively make sure that my ID was in my wallet at all times. I wasn't about to waste another day of my grandma's time.

The next exam day came. I was prepared with my kit, my ID, and my grandma. Nothing could go wrong. I had practiced over and over again.

I finally made it through the ID checking line, and the line to check in, and the line to be directed to our test stations, where we were finally sat. Students partaking in the exam could not speak to their models. We also did not know exactly what we were going to be tested on. There were twenty services that were options for the exam. Out of those twenty, there were twelve that we'd be tested on, and because we didn't know which twelve they would be, we had to be ready for anything.

The hours seemed to fly by. Perm wrap—check. Shampoo set—check. Haircut—check. Relaxer— not so check. As I was applying the relaxer service on my grandma, I ran out of time. I couldn't fucking believe it. When you run out of time on a part of the exam, you're immediately disqualified and have to reschedule to come back to take the service that you were disqualified on. This time I wasn't sad; this time I was furious with myself. I'd have to come back *again*.

My grandma looked at me, and I looked at her. She knew what had just happened, and although she was a little irritated, the look in her eyes said, "Well, we'll just come back."

The exam ended, and we left. Instead of tears, we had a good laugh about it.

"Gee, Andrea, maybe God's trying to tell you that you shouldn't do hair," my grandma laughed. She wasn't the devout Catholic my grandpa was, but she had enough faith in whatever was bigger than us to read signs from the universe.

"Grandma! Don't say that!" I laughed as I shifted my car into fourth gear on the way back to my dad's house.

A couple weeks later, exam day came once again. This time, I had my ID, I had practiced and practiced and practiced some more, and had my timing down to the second. I purposely timed myself to finish ahead so I wouldn't have to stress about running out of time.

Many times in my life, I've been grateful for my grandma Lorraine, but this time I was especially grateful for her. She'd driven thirty minutes three different times to make sure I succeeded and took my test. She never complained, which is unusual for her. She generally complains about everything, but for this, she didn't. She knew this was my future…and that this mattered. She always had faith in me and pushed me to push myself. I could have easily given up after the second flub-up, but I couldn't do that to her—or myself, for that matter.

I went through the same routine at the same exam site. We could now do this with our eyes closed. We sat in yet a different chair and had to wait until the relaxer segment of the exam was taking place. I had to believe that my career as a hairdresser would be far better than this experience.

The time came, and I finished the relaxer application within seventeen minutes (we were given twenty minutes). Relieved and ready to get out of there, I knew I had done it right this time, and I wouldn't have to return to the basement space in an old, dated mall with unflattering, fluorescent lighting. I could tell that my grandma knew it, too.

We wrapped up, I packed my kit, and we left. We chatted about this-and-that on the way back to my dad's house.

"Thank you, grandma." I hugged her as we parked.

"Sure thing. I hope you made it this time!" She grabbed her purse and stepped into her car.

"I think I did," I replied with confidence. "Call me when you get home."

She drove off, and once inside, I unloaded my kit, lit one of my dad's cigarettes, and opened a can of beer. He wasn't home from work yet, and today called for a beer and a smoke.

Two weeks later my cosmetology license came in the mail. I lit a cigarette, cracked open a beer, and immediately called my grandma.

"So when can you do my hair?" she asked.

A Date with the Mona Lisa

"Do you want to go to Paris?"

"What do you mean 'Do I want to go to Paris?'"

"I mean, do you want to go to Paris next month? I
have to know."

"Are you serious? I don't understand what you
mean."

"I won a trip for two to Paris, and I need to tell
them who I'm taking. Remember? I told you the
salon was having that retail contest? The prize
being a trip to Paris? I told you about it. I won it. I
just want to be back to go see Dad on the 17th,
obviously. So, do you want to go to Paris next
month?"

Sometimes the universe puts things in place right
when you need them. I had just broken off my

engagement with Derik in January, and he finally moved out of my condo on March 1st. I'd known about the trip for a while now. We were inching up on the one-year anniversary of our dad's passing, which is March 17th. He had left us some money that we were blowing through, yet were trying to be responsible with it. I was twenty-eight and Adrian, my little sister, was twenty-four. Our mother had proven to be a lunatic after our dad's passing. When we were little, we were just far enough apart in age that we never related to each other. Our grandma Lorraine used to always tell us, "All you have is each other." I'd always blow her comment off because I was perpetually irritated by my little sister. It would be unnatural not to be, right? And our parents, our mom specifically, always had a way of coddling her and making me feel guilty for any accomplishment that I had achieved because she somehow felt I owed that success to my little sister. "What's so hard about Adrian achieving her own success? Why must I be the one responsible for her?" I'd ask myself.

This made me incredibly resentful toward my sister, but I'd later find out that it wasn't her fault. Somehow, some way, I had gotten through all of the trauma, all of the darkness, and I had made a somewhat decent life for myself (I'd later figure out I had a very long, long way to go). It was my so-called decent life that, in turn, made my mother resentful toward me. She constantly applied guilt on me on behalf of my sister: not for my sister, but for herself. What parent wouldn't want to see their child become stable and successful? My mother. Or any mother who hadn't quite tried hard enough, worked hard enough, hadn't just let the divorce go, let her former life go, and hadn't had either the courage or know-how to start over. For her, it was much easier to complain and ask for money. The money thing always fell on my shoulders, and dealing with the emotional stuff was the part Adrian played in supporting our mother. The veil had been lifted for us after our mom's erratic behavior at our dad's funeral and her insistence on us giving her the money that our dad had left us. We'd later blow through it, and honestly, I wish I would have never had it. It was a burden, and it tore our family apart. And it certainly didn't bring my dad back from the dead.

Given the current tension between our mom and us, you could imagine her thoughts on the subject of us going to Paris. She'd immediately feel entitled to money, because, "if they have money for Paris, they have money for me." Little did she realize I had worked my ass off for over six months to achieve my goal of winning this trip to Paris. It, in fact, did not fall out of the sky. I earned it.

It wasn't until we were adults that Adrian and I finally became friends, confidants, family, and sisters.

Adrian was in her first real relationship with a guy named Tad. He was a privileged snot, and well, we just weren't cut from the same cloth. He always had a condescending way of making her feel stupidly insecure about who she was and where she came from. We'd never had the means to travel abroad when we were growing up. In fact, travel was never encouraged or talked about because it was out of reach for 'people like us'. So, I literally spent a great deal of my life thinking I could never achieve the luxury of travel. So did my sister. This is something that Tad held over Adrian's head to make her feel inadequate. I'm not convinced he did this on purpose, but he did it. He had an innate way of making her feel like she was diminutive. Now, her big sister was about to take her on a trip to Paris.

The salon held a retail contest consisting of one rule: sell the shit out of the French product we carry, and that product company will send you to Paris. So I worked my ass off….and won. I would win two more trips to Paris due to outstanding sales.

A couple weeks later, we packed our bags and were off to enjoy our first overseas adventure. We'd never been to Europe before. Our family vacations consisted of trips to the mountains. I wasn't even aware that travel was an option or a thing that people did until I was a teenager. No one in my family had the money to travel, and traveling was looked upon as something only the very privileged did. That most certainly was not us as we were growing up. I think our parents did their best, or the best they could do within their means, but traveling abroad was thought as something that would never happen to us. We weren't 'those people'.

After a connection in Dallas that we almost missed, we boarded our flight to CDG Paris and were off. The flight was long but welcomed by me. I drank an airplane-sized bottle of red wine and took a Tylenol PM. Lights out.

We landed at CDG and went through customs. The whole experience was so exhilarating. Hearing all of the different languages and seeing different languages was so new to us. We were actually here, in a place we never thought people like us would get to see. We even enjoyed the experience of grabbing a cab outside. Once we hopped in the Benz, we were finally ready to enjoy our Parisian adventure.

It was rainy and gloomy. The buildings, no doubt, contained tales that only buildings like that could tell. So old and historic yet contained an element of modernism. Everything was just a little bit more sophisticated, but it was the norm, from the Mercedes-Benz cabs to the cab drivers that wore either suits and ties or slacks and button-down shirts. The traffic was horrendous between CDL and Paris. Equally tired and excited after our long travels, we couldn't help but be in awe of what we were seeing for the first time. Passing the Arc De Triomphe was so monumental. It was our first time overseas, our first time in Europe, and we were experiencing it together.

The Benz taxi dropped us off at our hotel near the Marais district of Paris. It was raining and gloomy and as fabulous as we imagined Paris to be. The buildings were all the same color of muted tan-meets-jail grey, and were all about five stories tall. We entered our hotel, and said the customary, 'Bon jour;' however, without that much glee. We were jet-lagged and fried. I was dealing with my post-engagement breakup, had chopped off all my hair, was newly tattooed, and although I thought I really knew who I was, I had no fucking idea.

The gentleman at the desk of the tiny Parisian hotel was quite friendly and immediately recognized that we were Americans via our very American accents. He graciously spoke to us in English and showed us to our room. Contrary to popular American belief, the French aren't assholes. We are. Only in American culture do we have the arrogance and

237

expectation that everyone on the fucking planet should speak our language, accommodate our lack of bilingual skills, and do it with a fucking smile, and if they don't, well, then that whole country gets a bad rap. We are the greatest nation on the globe, after all, and the globe should accommodate us.

We arrived in our little room, and thank goodness, there were two twin beds. We each changed, brushed our teeth, and crashed. I'm a light sleeper, so into my ears my earplugs went. What seemed like just a few minutes was actually about four hours of sleep. We had crashed. I was oversleeping, and my sister had to wake me up. I felt like a zombie. It was like my dad's death, my engagement breakup with Derik, and our fighting with our mom had all sunk in and hit me the second we landed on French soil at CDG. I was emotionally depleted.

When we finally woke up, we were so giddy! We looked out the windows into the rain and loved the sound of the French police sirens. Everything was so different and cool and new and foreign to us. I was so proud to have worked so hard and been awarded this trip and to have been able to take my sister.

We decided to shower and hit the city. I told Adrian that I wanted to get tattooed in Paris. This would start my tradition of getting tattooed abroad. My tattoos are my permanent souvenirs and keepsakes.

Thankfully, my former boss and friend had marked some points of reference on a map for us. We followed that closely and began walking. How fucking cool was this!? We were in *Paris*, listening to everyone speak in different languages and seeing the charming chalk boards outside of cafes with the daily menu written in the handwriting you only see in Paris. After one trip to the ATM, we were ready to get our day going.

Leave it to us to have our first meal in the gayest of gay bar restaurants blaring American pop music. We had to crack up. We joked that our friend, Rodriguez, would be having a heyday over the cute Parisian waiters. We ordered sandwiches, which were underwhelming, and vowed only to eat at brasseries and cafes from now on in order to experience only the legit shit, none of this foofy, American-inspired crap. Although, the waiters were fun and funny, and my sister always felt at home in a gay bar.

We tromped around the city and quickly found a shoe store where we purchased our first pairs of French footwear. Oh, it was just so exciting. We were dressed cute and were so in awe of everything. We felt so international and refined. At these moments, I realized that this is what life is all about. It's about making memories with those who are closest to you. The simplicity of walking down the streets of Paris for the first time together and experiencing all that together and knowing that, in our hearts, our hearts felt the exact same thing.

We had lost our dad almost a year prior, and I had been in heavy therapy since. Our mom had become difficult, so it was like I lost both parents in one year. Adrian and I really needed each other. What we were experiencing now was so contradictory to what the past had brought us, our dad dying as an addict and alcoholic and all of the deep-rooted and dark realities that came with that. We'd both worked really hard to overcome a lot of the cards that were dealt to us, and in a way neither of us felt deserving of this trip. European travel was for rich white people with money, not for people like us, not for working class people who struggle and live paycheck to paycheck...or so we had been taught to believe. It took me a very long time to realize and accept that I am, in fact, very deserving of a beautiful, healthy life, European travel and all.

We shopped and visited cafes and now it was time to get tattooed. Tattoos on the French, at least at the time, were a little frowned upon and taboo. The French are very proper and tattoos aren't as mainstream. That didn't stop me from wanting a tattoo.

We were able to find a tattoo parlor in the neighborhood near St. Germain. Down the little allies we went, and we literally stumbled upon it. We walked in, and it was very much like an American tattoo shop, right down to the sound, the music, the lighting, and the art.

"Bon jour!" we greeted the gentleman working the desk. We'd soon learn not to greet people with this much enthusiasm. It's more customary to be a little more subdued.

"Bon jour, mademoiselle. How are you today?" Again, our American accents rang through like a fire alarm.

"Doing well, thank you. I'm interested in getting a tattoo if anyone is available."

"Yes, of course. What would you like?"

"How do you say and spell 'sister' in French?"

"Soeur."

"I'd like that on my left wrist."

"Andi, get it in red ink," my sister piped in.

"I was thinking purple, but purple fades so fast." She knew right away the purple was a Prince reference. We'd grown up on Prince; our parents listening to him day in and day out.

"Well, maybe get a dove. For 'When Doves Cry'." She was literally thinking what I was thinking.

'I'll get that when I get home." I said. There was already a language barrier, and I didn't want to push it. About a month after our trip, I had a dove added to my tattoo.

She was touched that I was getting 'sister' tattooed on my left wrist. It seemed like the only option. It was appropriate seeing how we'd become so much closer, and this was our first time oversees and we were in Paris together. Yes, 'sister' was perfect. It was meaningful and would forever commemorate our trip to Paris.

We followed the heavily pierced and tattooed Frenchman into one of the rooms. He had to translate to the artist what I wanted: the word 'soeur' in red ink written in cursive on my left wrist. Easy. I had gotten 'Dad' tattooed on my right wrist a few weeks after he had died. I would later learn from a close friend who is also an intuitive medium that the left side is our receiving side. Our right side is our letting-go side. I didn't know this at the time, but how suiting was that?

The tattoo took all of about seven minutes to complete. The artist was a French kid with a shaved head and the prettiest blue eyes I had ever seen. He had the most detailed tattoo of the Blessed Mother tattooed on his arm. He said he got it in Brazil.

We left the shop, and continued gallivanting around St. Germain. This would quickly become my favorite Parisian neighborhood next to Le Halle and the Marias. Walking around Paris with its infectious energy, cafes, beautiful people, shops, and endless little streets was like walking in a dream. Adrian and I were having the time of our lives, and we'd only been in Paris for about ten hours. We'd shopped, ate, laughed, gotten tattooed, taken pictures, and we were hungry.

My sister and I always have the best luck when we're traveling. We stumble upon the greatest restaurants. With our hands full of shopping bags, we went into a restaurant that was, like many restaurants, advertising prix fixe meals on their chalkboards outside. Roasted lamb was listed, and since that's my second favorite animal to eat, we went in and were seated.

Much to our advantage, we don't look American, and so we were often treated like Europeans. This was in 2008 when Bush was in his last months of the administration, and well, the whole world pretty much hated the United States. We were thankful for our dark, non-American features. They served us well at that time.

As we sat, we noticed the table next to us. Seated there were a few French guys, probably around our age. Now, I was just out of an engagement and being single and available hadn't quite registered yet. One of the guys was cute, and another was bald and had a nice smile and gigantic blue eyes. Adrian and I ate our delicious prix fixe lamb and shared a bottle of wine.

One of the gentlemen from the table next to us approached our table. He had overheard our English, so he spoke to us in English.

"Um, hello. How are you this evening? We heard you at our table and are wondering if you'd like to join us at a jazz club around the corner after dinner?"

Adrian and I shared glances and I replied, "We're really well this evening. Thank you for asking. How are you? We'd like to go to the jazz club, but we have our shopping bags with us."

"Not a problem." These are very popular words amongst the French and happen to be three of my favorite words. They had a solution for just about everything. "You bring your bags. We go to the jazz club and have a good time."

"Okay! We have to pay our bill. Then we can go."

"Very good."

The Frenchman with the shaved, bald head and huge blue eyes had come over to the table now and asked if we were joining them. He was delighted we were.

Being the well-mannered culture the French are, the boys picked up our shopping bags and carried them down the street to the jazz club.

"You're not going to steal our shit, are you?" I asked half joking, half not. I'd just spent a pretty penny at Cop Copine in St. Germain, and I'd be pissed if our new friends jacked us for our new clothes.

"Don't be ridiculous! What? You think we are going to wear your clothes? Ha!" One of them replied. The one with the blue eyes and bald head seemed to be rather taken with me, the one with dark hair was eyeing my sister, and the other one was along for the ride and was having a good time with his friends and the two American girls they'd picked up at the restaurant.

"Maybe! What if you take our shit?" I laughed. This was fun, joking around with new friends on a Parisian night on our way to a jazz club. It doesn't get any more Parisian than that.

The gentleman opened the door to the jazz club. It was dark and packed and smoky. The room was small and smelled of cigarettes, red wine, and something reminiscent of an old library book. There was an attractive black woman on stage singing in French and a man playing a snare, one playing a bass, and another playing a sax. The singer's energy was sultry and sexy. She had flawless skin, a perm that made her hair appear more natural than it would at its collarbone length, and her lips were the color of vin rouge. The chairs were packed very closely together, and there were tiny tables sporadically spread around the room with just enough room on them to house a few glasses of wine and an ashtray.

Adrian and I were thrilled. Our new friends led us to a few seats, shopping bags and all. We ordered vin rouge and sat and enjoyed the show. We were all feeling a little chatty, so we headed over to an open booth to talk and laugh and drink and smoke.

The bald, blue-eyed one named Gerard sat next to me. As my sister was chatting and laughing with the other guys and telling them of her half-French boyfriend, Gerard was talking to me.

"What do you do back in the United States?"

"I'm a hairdresser. That's how we got here. There's a French product that we sell, and I sold the most of it during a contest and won this trip to Paris and took my sister."

"Fantasteek! Very nice! You must do very well. Welcome to Paris. What have you guys seen so far? How long is your holiday?" I love how Europeans say "holiday", as opposed to "vacation".

"We just arrived today. We were in St. Germain most of the day and are staying close to the Marais. We shopped and walked around, and I got tattooed."

"Tattooed! You got tattooed? What did you get?"

I showed him my new tattoo.

"Ahhh. Soeur. Sister. Very nice. Did she get one as well?"

"No! She didn't!" I said.

"Adrian! You passed on getting a tattoo?" Gerard asked as he took a large sip of vin rouge.

"Yeah, I remove tattoos for a living, and red is the hardest ink to remove," she said as she sipped her wine.

"Thanks for telling me that! Not that I'm going to get it removed, but shit. You don't get a matching tattoo, *and* you suggest the hardest ink color to remove!?"

She wasn't paying attention. Gerard and I continued our conversation.

"Are you from Paris?"

"No. I'm from Lyon. I'm here for the day for work, and I'm heading back in the morning. My friends live here, and we went to eat dinner and now here we are with you guys."

"You have to take the train to Lyon in the morning? Aren't you going to be tired?"

"Ahhh, it's life! It's fun! I'm young. I'll sleep on the train."

"You're right about that! Fuck it. Live. Life is too short."

The guys were ready to go. It was late, and Gerard and his brunette friend insisted on taking a cab with us to the hotel. As we approached our hotel, Gerard asked what room we were in. I told him, joking that he better not be a murderer or something. Adrian and I went up to our room, and within minutes, the phone rang. We looked at each other in shock, and she answered.

"Hello?"

She handed me the phone. I was perplexed.

"Hello?"

"Andrea! It's Gerard. I'm in a taxi. Join me. I'm downstairs. I want to show you the city."

I mouthed to Adrian what he'd said and she mouthed back: *go!*

"Okay. Let me gather my things, and I'll be right down." Was this for real? A cute French guy we met at dinner wanted to take me on a drive around the city of Paris? Right now?

"Andi, just go. Have fun. You haven't had fun in a really long time. You deserve it. Just be careful." My sister knew how unhappy I was in my engagement, and how deprived I was of spontaneity and having fun. She was right. I was going to go on a drive with a Frenchman around the city of Paris because, well, why the fuck not?

Gerard opened the door to the taxi for me and told the driver that we'd be driving around for a while. I could decipher a little bit of what he said, but he told the driver to take us to the Eiffel Tower, Moulin Rouge, The Louvre, and the Arc de Triomphe.

Paris at night is incredible. It's called The City of Lights for very good reason. Paris at night and Paris during the day are two different worlds. Although old and historic and aged during the day with just the right amount of city hardness to it, Paris becomes softer and more romantic t night. The lights glow and bounce off the river that flows through the city; The Seine. The Eiffel Tower is even more opulent and magnificent at night. The entire city becomes romantic and illuminated. Driving past Moulin Rouge and the Louvre at night gave me a sense of just how grand and multifaceted

Paris is. During the day, you stumble upon tiny roads and hidden gems of cafes and shops. At, night all of the spectacles of Paris are illuminated and the tourists are long gone, or at least they were at 3:00 a.m. when we passed the Arc de Triomphe.

Gerard told the driver to let us out on the Champs Elysees. The Champs is a long road—and quite the tourist cluster fuck during the day. At night, it was the perfect place for Gerard to grab my hand and kiss me. What a good kisser. Would I sleep with him? Probably not. I'm not the one-night-stand kind of person. I know myself better than that. I get attached, and all of my sexual issues resurface with monogamous sex, and pretty much take over whenever I've had casual sex.

"Let's go to the disco over here. We'll dance and have a good time! And we'll kiss more." In less than twenty-four hours in Paris, I'd slept the best I'd slept in almost a year, had a phenomenal meal with my sister, gotten tattooed, purchased French fashions, met new friends, visited a jazz club, and now was making out with a Frenchman as he took me on a tour of the city at night in a Mercedes Benz taxi.

We walked into the club, and it was jam-packed full of people. The French really love American pop music, so I had to settle for that. It certainly wasn't my first choice.

"What would you like to drink?" he shouted in my ear over the loud music while grabbing my ass. I've always had a bit of an ass. I used to be ashamed of it; it was then that I started to embrace it. The French seemed to appreciate it. At least Gerard did.

"Vodka soda!" I shouted back as he kissed me.

He returned with a sippy cup full of warm apple juice and vodka. Europeans don't do ice that much, and apple juice is a regular mixer. I had to laugh, but after my first sip out of the sippy cup with a straw, I didn't think the taste of hot apple juice was that appetizing. I eventually choked it down.

We didn't dance much. We found a dark booth and made out the whole time. I could feel his hard dick under his pants. I hadn't had sex in a few months and didn't really want to do the one-night thing, but this making out in a dark booth in a Parisian nightclub was fun, to say the least. After a while, we decided to leave. It was even later than we thought, but things in Paris don't close until the sun comes up. Even then, clubs are still open. We walked through the crowd of drunk, dancing club-goers, and headed out the door where Gerard hailed us a cab.

We got back to the hotel where Adrian and I were staying, and he came in with me. We weren't done with each other yet. In French, he told the man at the desk that he wanted a room. The man looked at me, looked at him, realized I was already staying there, then looked at him again and slid him a key to a room across the wood desk.

Gerard took my hand and led me to the elevator where we continued our make-out session, and he didn't stop until he picked me up and carried me to the room. He turned the TV on to the French equivalent of MTV. The downtempo beats of Fiest were on; setting the mood. Off went most of our clothes. I was feeling more confident in my body at that time. As soon as I ended my engagement, I dropped about ten pounds. I no longer looked pudgy and thick. I had my shape back, and my tummy had flattened out. I was now proud of my body, as opposed to being embarrassed of it.

Within minutes, his face was in my pussy. I loved getting my pussy eaten but had never come from it. At that time, I had only come from intercourse, but if you want to suck on my clit, I'm not going to stop you. If you want to finger me and hit my g-spot, I'm not going to stop you, either. But in order for me to cum on your dick, you're going to have to fuck me right. At that moment, I may have slept with him. I mean, we were doing everything else. I reciprocated the oral pleasure and made him cum. Once insecure about my blowjob abilities, I eventually enlisted the help of a gay coworker on how to give good head and was thoroughly educated. I had to learn when I met Derik. He loved sex and getting head more than life itself, and I wasn't confident in my skills. Learn from a gay man if you want to know how to make a guy's eyes cross and his body quiver like the aftershock of an earthquake. Gerard had to settle for that because I wouldn't let him fuck me, and we didn't have protection. I didn't get off, but still felt alive and satisfied. It wouldn't be till years later that I'd be able to get off from oral and getting fingered. I also couldn't climax if I had been drinking, and in order for me to really release and let go, I have to have a deep connection with someone. I wouldn't learn this until I was thirty-six.

We laid there naked for a while, and the time had come for him to catch his train. I was sleepy, no longer feeling the effects of warm apple juice and vodka, and wanted to shower and go to bed. It was around 9:00 am, and he had a two-hour train ride to Lyon.

We left the room. I was in a daze over what just happened. It seemed too surreal, but at the same time it seemed like it was exactly what was meant to be. I bid him farewell, and he did give me his number. This was before the age of the accessibility of social media where we could have started following each other right then and there. I knew I'd never see him again, even though I wouldn't be opposed to it. I watched him grab a cab, and he blew me a kiss from the window.

I opened the door to the room and let my sister continue sleeping. I took a cat nap, and then we both awoke and got ready. We had a date with the Mona Lisa.

He Has The Most Perfect Cock

When a client sees me every four to eight weeks for their hair, the relationship becomes one built on a foundation of me tending to the beauty needs of the client, and the client needing to vent and talk about personal matters in a confidential setting. I can bet my life on it that clients confide in their hairdressers more than they do their significant others, their best friends, and maybe even their therapists.

When a client sits in their stylist's chair, an instant connection is formed based on trust, instinct, and having one's needs met. The client/stylist relationship is one that is very intimate. The stylist is, after all, physically touching the client, reading into their insecurities, needs, wants, and determining how to fix said insecurities to the best of their hairdresser's abilities, all while trying to please the client and their desires.

Often, the client is lacking self-confidence, going through a breakup or divorce, or searching for their dream job all the while, desiring the confidence to feel like a better version of themselves—or maybe they just want to look fucking hot. They need the faith in themselves to be able to walk into that office and land their dream job, or accidentally/on purpose bump into their ex looking better than ever. It's my job to make you look good and feel even better. Once this task is achieved by the stylist, you've gained life-long trust from the client. If you bless your client with a flawless haircut and new hair color that is capable of haunting her ex with regret for the rest of his living days that he fucked her over by fucking her best friend, well, you've got job security.

Eva started seeing me when she was still in high school, right around the time my diet consisted of cocaine, ecstasy, vodka, and breakfast burritos. We'd always had a fun bond. We were both young, and going through, seemingly, the same shit at the same time: relationships, traveling, partying, more traveling, more partying, and somehow living to tell and laugh about it.

Given our long history, it's safe to say that I'm probably one of the few people that Eva really confided in. And years later, close to my retirement from hairdressing, she became someone I could confide in, too. She'd always remained private— only a few select people knew her like I did.

She was just out of a relationshit, (that's my term for a shitty relationship), and unbeknownst to me, I was just around the corner from getting my heart broken once again by a guy that was over ten years younger than me. Go figure.

At one appointment, she divulged that she'd been having casual sex with a friend of a friend. She was doing the typical rebound thing to get over the bastard that had just blown her off and who failed to mention that he had a girlfriend on the side for the last three months of their relationship, or relationshit. So, in typical form, she needed some good dick.

"Andi. Oh. My. God. He has the most perfect fucking cock," Eva said with much enthusiasm.

"Don't you love that? They're not all perfect, that's for fucking sure," I agreed as I applied color to her roots.

"No. You don't understand. Like, it's fucking perfect. I mean, we're just hooking up right now, you know? But his dick fits me perfectly."

"You're not going to catch the feelings are you?" I looked at her over my glasses.

"Fuck no, dude. Are you fucking kidding me? I just want to get my brains fucked out." Eva took a swig of her latte.

"Who doesn't?! Last night, I swear to God, I came in Gabe's mouth three times... *three*," I said, agreeing, that yes, most of us like to get our brains fucked out from time to time. I also had to add that I was receiving the best oral I'd ever had—*ever*.

"It sucks. He's not responding to me, and I'm going out of town in three days. Is it too much to ask for a good dicking before I go to LA? Oh! Dude! Aiden used to make me cum in his mouth every fucking time. It's a gift, really." I nodded in agreement. A guy can either make you cum in his mouth or not. I suggest moving on if it's the latter.

"I think you deserve a good dicking. Text him again, and tell him just that. He'll respond. I guarantee. Can I tell you that I came to work with cum on my pants the other day? I, too, had just received a good dicking from Gabe, and apparently didn't check my pants. Honest to shit, I pulled up to work at 8:00 am, went to unfasten my seatbelt, looked down, and there was dried cum on my pants. I had to hurry up and try to wash it out and put my apron over it. Of course, my first client that day was my uber-conservative Christian client. I felt like such a whore." Eva laughed at me. I laughed at myself.

At Eva's next appointment, I had bad news about Gabe and I, and she was growing ever leery of her fuck buddy. She was also catching some feelings for him.

"It all goes down from there. When we start feeling shit. God damn feelings," I said. I was a little down. Gabe was pulling the predictable distant shit guys pull. This distance was conveniently taking place a week after he told me he was in love with me. And I was in love with him. I was confused and hurt but trying not to show it. It was all too familiar. Vulnerability isn't exactly my strong suit, so the distance was a pain that was penetrating deep into the familiar territory of abandonment and rejection from men. And it was agonizing.

"Andi, it's bullshit. You know? What the fuck? I haven't heard from that motherfucker, either. I mean, I know we're just hooking up, but still. I can't get a text back?" Eva was also a little down and bothered.

"That's why I can't do casual. I learned that a long time ago. Believe it or not, I'm too emotional. I get attached. Then I get sad. And let me fucking tell you, I've done shit with and to Gabe that I've *never* done with anyone else, and now he fucking pulls this shit? He was in love with me a month ago? What the fuck? Do they just spew that out of their mouths? It takes a lot for me to do that shit with a guy. You know? Like, I have to feel something deep and have a genuine connection and chemistry. You think I suck dick like that for just *anyone?* Shit, he needs a nap and a hit off a blunt after I make him cum in my mouth. That's how good I am. That motherfucker is privileged. And he doesn't even realize it." Truth be told, I was experiencing some PTSD from my heartbreak from my relationship with Sam from a few years earlier. Heartbreak PTSD can haunt you at any moment. It was all resurfacing.

"I know. Maybe I can't do casual, either." Eva's phone went off. She paused and turned red.

"It's Aiden." Aiden was the ex that had a girlfriend while he was seeing her. Aiden was the ex that she was currently rebounding from with a friend of a friend. Aiden was also the guy whose mouth she had frequently cum in.

I almost dropped my color brush. "Are you fucking kidding me?"

"Andi, he hasn't hit me up in over six months."

"Six months!? Are you going to text him back?"

"Fuck no I'm not going to text him back! Not until my hair is done and I feel fabulous!" Eva took another swig of her sparkling water and slammed her phone down.

"I wonder what he wants?" I said as I pulled the red hair dye through the ends of her shoulder-length hair.

"It's like they have fucking radar. Here I am, getting the best dick of my life, not thinking about him in weeks, and he fucking hits me up. What in the fuck?"

"He knows you're over it. Are you over it?" I finish applying her color and put my rubber gloves on my station.

"I mean, yeah, I guess. You know? He had a fucking girlfriend for three fucking months while we dated. What does he want after doing that to me?" I could tell this struck a chord. Her energy shifted. All the good dick in the world isn't capable of stitching up the wound of betrayal.

During her eyebrow wax we rehearsed how she'd respond.

"I think you should ask what his intentions are by him contacting you. The last time you guys talked was when you found out about that chick." I ripped the wax off along with her excess eyebrow hairs. I could tell she was bothered and would be for a while. This is the thing with being a hairdresser for a client for so long: you begin to read each other. She wasn't just a client anymore; she was a friend. And I cared about her and her feelings, and I didn't want to see that undeserving snake hurt her feelings again. Since I see her once a month for her regular hair appointment, I had seen the damage and repair she'd just gone through. It was beginning to resurface. All it took was one text of, "Hey, how are you?" to bring it all flooding back.

I shampooed the color out of her hair and gave her an extra fancy blow-out to boost her mood and confidence. When we look good, we feel good, right?

Eva nervously checked out of the salon and assured me she'd text me with the outcome. I told her to stay strong and maybe get some dick from her fuck buddy if that would make her feel better. She said it might and texted him straight away.

Four weeks later, Eva was back for her root touch-up.

"I never did hear from my fuck buddy again. What the fuck? Aiden hits me up only to tell me he saw some t-shirt he thought I'd like, and my fuck buddy blows me off. How does one get blown off by a fuck buddy!?" Eva was feeling rejected and in the dumps. I was too, as Gabe and I had drifted into an ambiguous place, and I didn't like it. I was hurt.

"Aiden hit you up to tell you about a fucking t-shirt? I call bullshit. He wants to see you." I was stirring her color. My back was already starting to hurt, a common plight of being a hairdresser. Especially after twenty years.

"You think?"

"Yes! Come on. Guys are not that ballsy. He was feeling you out." I began applying the red hair dye to her dirty blonde roots.

"I mean, I only responded kind of distantly. He responded to me, but I never responded to him. Why should I? I did see on Facebook that he and that chick broke up. That's why he's hitting me up, but I want no part of it. He lied to me straight to my face about having a fucking girlfriend on the side. Fuck that. He can fuck the fuck off." Clearly she was still pissed about the situation...and rightfully so.

This is the thing with modern relationships and dating. Everything is via text message or a 'like' on a social media platform. Everyone exposes their everything to the world on social media. A gifted social media stalker can find out who is dating who, and if so-and-so 'likes' this or that person's status at any given moment. Often in the minds of the modern-day dater, frequent 'likes' from one person to another means that they're in a relationship already.

The art of communicating and expressing ones' feelings to one another has slipped through the cracks. In the good old days, we'd actually pick up the phone or speak in person about how and what we were feeling. Now, we're left to decipher social media statuses and memes to see if there was a subliminal message or hint as to what our current love interest is thinking or doing. This is what Eva was doing with her fuck buddy, since he'd dropped off the face of the earth and all. She needed some sort of clue as to where he'd gone, and what he was doing.

Is this sort of thing considered stalking? Of course. In modern day dating, when you're not getting the answers you need from the person you need them from, you're left to do some detective work. Sometimes you find you were overacting, and sometimes you find the truth: necessary closure. In Eva's case, this is how she found out that Aiden had a girlfriend on the side. He'd been tagged in a picture of the girlfriend—lips locked at a concert.

The back-and-forth of text messaging and all of the game playing that comes along with dating are another beast entirely. If he or she doesn't text back within a reasonable amount of time, then, well, they must certainly be fucking someone else.

I know Eva well enough to know that even though she tried not to show it too much, she was hurt again. The agony of rejection is a tough pill to swallow. I too was swallowing the pill of rejection once again with Gabe.

A month later, she came in for her routine touch-up. This was also our last appointment together. I was retiring from my career as hairdresser after twenty and a half years. I had relayed the news to my clients about a month prior. Due to unforeseen circumstances with our lease at the salon, the owner decided to close. I took this as a sign, along with my mental and physical burnout, that it was time to retire as a hairdresser. It had been almost twenty-one years.

"This is bullshit. This isn't goodbye! We're going to go out and be fabulous and be the unicorns we are, have brunches and go dancing," Eva proclaimed as she walked into the salon with a bouquet of flowers and a box of gluten-free cookies. She gave me a long hug.

"That's right! Fuck no. This isn't goodbye! I've been doing your hair for, what, almost seventeen years!?" I hugged her back, and then took a bite of a cookie.

Eva sat down and I begin applying her color for the last time.

"How's it going? What's going on? Any word from the fuck buddy? Or did he puss out for good?" I asked, eating another gluten-free cookie.

"No! I never heard from that motherfucker again! And I caught the feels, damn it! When the 'D' is so good, things just get jumbled up inside." She drank from her whiskey-spiked latte. As a now-sober person, I can smell alcohol a mile away.

"When did men stop being men? That's what it is. They can't just fucking man up and tell you they don't want to see you anymore. They do it by not responding to you anymore. They just ignore you or all of a sudden turn off their feelings with a flick of an internal "I'm being a pussy" switch. It's bullshit." I was a little fired up. Gabe had not responded to a text of mine from over a week ago, and out of nowhere, was suddenly the selfie-king of social media. He could post pictures of himself, but couldn't respond to me.

"They're pussies. All of them. I tell you what, I'm going to New York next week, and I'm hitting up my 'friend.'" If he's single and I'm single, we always hook up. He goes down on me for hours. I bought some super sexy bras and panties," Eva said as she crossed her legs and opened an app on her phone. I think it was a dating app.

"Good for you. Get your crotch eaten out. I'm too fragile for any of that right now. That fucker." I was referencing Gabe as I took a half-inch off her dry ends.

"Andi, we're a catch. You know? We're good women. We have our heads on straight, we don't have kids or baby daddy baggage. We're smart, driven, hot, and fun. What the fuck? Why is it so hard to find anyone to date?" Eva asked.

"I don't fucking know, dude. I mean, I'm a good person. I have my shit together. I'm not perfect, but I'd never just dip out with no explanation. I've got bigger balls than these motherfuckers, you know? Shit, I'm a fucking catch. I'm thirty-six, I have no kids, no ex-husband. I'm independent; I'm well-read; I've traveled; I have a home; I can cook; I can fuck; and I shave my legs every day. This shit does not exist!" I was done applying her color for the very last time. We'd been lamenting and having similar conversations during her hair appointments. It donned on me that this was last time we'd have this conversation in the salon. That this client-hairdresser level of trust and intimacy would no longer happen in my life. At that moment, it hit me that my career as a hairdresser was rapidly ticking away.

"No shit! Fuck this. Let's move." We often spoke of moving away.

I dried Eva's hair for the last time, but we promised to go out and do brunch. And we would. Over the past seventeen years, Eva became not only a friend, but family.

"Okay. Text me this week," I said, hugging her, trying not to get choked up. My last day as a hairdresser was a few days away, and all of the goodbyes were starting to sink in. But this wasn't goodbye. This was the beginning of a new chapter in our friendship.

"Okay, I will. Thank you, Andi! I love it as always!" Eva walked out the door, and I went to the backroom to open the card she gave me with the flowers and cookies.

Embossed in gold foil, the front of the card read: "Stay Awesome Forever". I laughed a little to myself.

The inside read:

'You are an amazing unicorn of a woman and I can't wait to see what you do next. Keep being the beautiful, inspiring boss bitch that you are. There is no turning back. We are friends for life.

Love,

Eva

I shed a few tears. I had no idea I'd inspired anyone, let alone someone like Eva. She is fearless and fun and funny and always accepted people for who they are. She, quite honestly, inspired me. We'd grown up together, really. A lot had happened in those seventeen years of our client/stylist relationship turned friendship. So much so that it donned on me: you never know who you're inspiring through all of your trials and tribulations and lessons and the bouncing back from this or that. I had no idea I'd meant that much to her as a friend and hairdresser. I just hope she knows what she means to me.

And I hope her former fuck buddy and her ex both know what they missed out on. But they probably don't. Clearly they weren't smart enough to keep her around, let alone realize how much of a unicorn *she* is.

The Human Element

As a hairdresser, there is an unrealistic expectation put upon us not only by the industry, but by our clients and superiors. We're not allowed to have a bad day. We don't have the ability to shut our office door and zone out on our computer. We have to listen to what the client wants, listen to their life crisis, listen to their displeasure should they not like what we did to their hair last time. This is an incredible amount of pressure. Why, you ask? Because we have to do all of this while performing a service that our clients are paying top dollar for. Top dollar prices come with an expectation of perfection, not only in regard to the service, but also to the stylist as an individual. It's expected that we are dressed fashionably from head to toe, that our makeup is impeccable, and our hair is cutting edge. It's also expected that no matter how late a client is, or how shitty of a mood they are in, that we greet them with a smile, go above and beyond with our craft, and listen to their shit.

So, when people ask me why I retired at such a young age, I have to tilt my head in a little bit of confusion. I started my career when I was sixteen years old and was still attending high school. Twenty years of anything will lead to inevitable burnout and exhaustion. I'd be lying if I said it didn't lead to a little bit of resentment, too. Working with and on humans for twenty years will inevitably result in just that.

Aside from the obvious elements of learning and perfecting my craft over a span of two decades, I learned a lot about the human element. People really do tell their hairdressers everything. What I learned the most from people is that people cave into societal pressures, especially women. And it makes them unhappy—most of them, anyway.

I've always been of the school of thought that if you make a choice to have a family, you can't complain about it. I think I get that from my grandma. She instilled the opinion in me that nobody owes you anything if you choose to have a family and get married. It's what you chose, so now you have to live with your choice. If only it were that simple. I've chosen not to have children, and I live a very fulfilling and satisfying life. Children make a lot of people happy, as does marriage. But marriage and children make even *more* people unhappy. I know this for a fact because I have twenty years of experience under my belt of listening to people complain about their choices to get married and procreate.

It astonished me—really—after all these years, to learn that. From my experience, I think I can safely say that well over half of people who are married and have children are unhappy. I think that's really sad. I've had countless clients tell me they secretly envy my life and wish they would have done things differently. I find that tragic. What if your husband or wife or kids knew that you regretted having them in your life and that you only

287

married your wife or husband and had both of your kids because that's what society says you should do? That you really aren't in love with your partner; they just look good on paper and said 'yes' because they figured time was of the essence.

I had a very successful client of mine tell me once that she hated playing with her sons at the end of a long day. She told me she's so tired and bored with her life that she wished her husband, whom she's not attracted to anymore, would just play with them so she wouldn't have to. It floors me that people can be so selfish that they bring other humans into their lives without really wanting them. I suggested she start saving for their therapy because her sons are going to need it. Kids are more intuitive than we give them credit for. After all, we all know when we're not wanted.

I had many good conversations with my clients, but it only takes a couple of draining people to send you over the edge and make you doubt what you do for a living. People think it's okay to come in with their bad moods, constant complaints about their lives, and then knit pick at their hair. When people ask me why I retired, I lie and say it was too physically demanding, when in all reality, I had had my fill of listening to people complain. I had also realized during the final few years of my career that doing hair was no longer my purpose. That I *was* capable of more than what I was doing. I learned that I like to write, I learned that I love to work out and go dancing, and, I even like doing accounting work. I'd learned a lot about myself in twenty years. Many people stay stuck, but I chose to keep evolving and moving forward. I chose to shed past versions of myself – and I chose to be okay with that. High-end fashion, designer drinks, trendy bars and restaurants – those were once part of my identity. I spent a fortune on those things, only to look back years later thinking of all of the other things I could have done with my vodka budget. But you live and you learn. And you can't put a price on life experience, yet alone a twenty-year long career by the age of thirty-six.

In addition to the draining conversations, along with it comes the whole aspect of people not respecting your time. When I realized that not only was I not living up to my potential, but I was also sacrificing a lot of valuable time and money while doing so. Reality really sunk in that at some point I would have to retire from doing hair. In the industry, if I'm not working on a client, I'm not getting paid, simple as that. So, when a client cancels less than a day, or even a day and a half prior to their appointment, I'm fucked. As a self-employed hairdresser, I had both a professional and personal bottom line I had to meet. If a client (mind you it was always the same clients with the same excuses) cancels an appointment even a day in advance, it's difficult to fill that time. Most of my work was color work, so my appointments took longer, meaning more time was scheduled. If I had blocked out two hours for a client, and, like clockwork, some sort of life event came up for the seventieth consecutive time and she had to cancel, I'm wasn't only out the money I would have made during that appointment, but I was also in the hole because I had to purchase the color to do the service. Given that this is the service industry, it is a little expected that these things come up. However, what people don't understand is that this was my livelihood. A few cancellations within a couple of weeks makes a dent in both my professional and personal obligations.

After receiving a text from my co-worker on the day before my work week was to begin telling me a certain client had called and left a message over the weekend cancelling her appointment for the following day, I decided I was done. I had been patient for a very long time. Had I been a wreck for a large portion of my career? Yes. Did I hide it well? Fuck yeah, I did. So well, that when I was finally comfortable with telling clients I had quit drinking, most of them were in shock and had zero clue I even drank at all. Regardless of my hidden hangovers, no one deserves to have their livelihood fucked with. I know it was never intentional when my clients put a dent in my income by cancelling and moving appointments around, but it did affect my livelihood. And, by age thirty-six, I had had enough. Not only that, but I was more than ready to dive in with both feet into the unknown. I'd had countless personal transitions, but this would be my first professional transition. I was more excited than scared.

At the end of my hairdresser chapter, I was mentally, physically, and emotionally drained. I dreaded coming to work and leaving with throbbing legs. I began to dread when certain clients were scheduled, knowing they'd complain about life for two hours. That's a long time to listen to someone complain about the weather and their in-laws. Luckily, this was often balanced out by fun and jovial conversations with more delightful clients, but add that up over twenty years, and it equals burnout. It equals being depleted from days and years of dispensing endless energy, physical work, and ongoing accommodation to people. Yes, it is what I chose to do. Did I love it? Of course. But it is natural for things to run their course. And that's okay. We have to let things run their course in order to see what is around the bend.

As soon as I announced my retirement via email and social media, I cried. Although I was ready, it was the biggest letting go of letting go that had occurred in my life. My longest relationship was my career. Even with the pain-in-the-ass clients that I had to deal with, I became incredibly attached to many of them. We became attached to each other. We knew each other better than our families did. That is nothing to blink an eye at. We were there for each other for all our major life events. You name it, and we lived it.

Whether they knew it or not, my clients were there with me when I was young and wild, when I was voted as one of the city's most eligible bachelorettes at the age of twenty-four by a local magazine; they were there when I was engaged, then disengaged. They were there when my dad died, when I got sober, when I had my first major heartbreak, and when I flew to Europe for the first time. These people were there for it all. And I thank them from the bottom of my heart for staying with me and letting me do their hair. I thank them for a career most would feel blessed to have accomplished. I thank them for the laughs and for the conversations we shared. I thank them for being a part of my story...even the ones that were a pain in the ass.

Epilogue

The stories in this book are ones that particularly stood out to me during my journey as a hairdresser. The drug and alcohol abuse was very much a part of my journey. As I write this, I've now been clean and sober for close to seven years.

As I look back on my career and what I accomplished, getting clean and sober was my biggest feat. I can't lie, winning trips to Paris and being in magazines and on a TV show are up there, but as far as what has made the most difference in my life, I have to say it was gaining a clear head and spirit.

I went through a lot during my career, most of which I never shared publicly until now. Sure, there are the funny stories of drunken nights and crazy clients, but I really did have a hidden struggle. Forcing myself to put on a smile day after day during some of my most trying times seemed nearly impossible. Coming back to work two weeks after my dad had died was a torture I'd never want to relive. Being around a group of seasoned partiers while getting sober led me to cry every day after work for three months straight.

Taking a stroll down memory lane to complete this project made me realize that I did accomplish a lot—that given my circumstances that shaped my life, I could have turned out to be a statistic, a life-long alcoholic, or dead. But something in me drove me to be more than that. Maybe I've wanted to do what my parents weren't able to do. Maybe I had to be a survivor because that has been my only option for most of my life. It doesn't matter. What matters is I made it; I survived.

I'm often asked: "So, now what are you going to do?". In all honesty, I have no idea. Letting go of a piece of yourself that is a twenty-year dent in your existence is overwhelming. But that's the best part. Letting go to let in is how we grow and learn about ourselves. Change is scary. But being completely open to the unknown is exhilarating. I've purposely let go of many of my anchors that were weighing me down and keeping me from my purpose. What is that purpose? I'm not exactly sure, but I think it starts with this book and includes more dates with the Mona Lisa.